T5-BPY-337

Library of
Davidson College

A Garland Series

ROMANTIC CONTEXT: POETRY

Significant Minor Poetry
1789-1830

Printed in photo-facsimile
in 128 volumes

selected and arranged by
Donald H. Reiman
The Carl H. Pforzheimer Library

William Lisle Bowles

Hope, an Allegorical Sketch

St. Michael's Mount

Song of the Battle of the Nile

The Sorrows of Switzerland

The Picture

Bowden Hill

The Grave of the Last Saxon

Ellen Gray

with an introduction
for the Garland edition by
Donald H. Reiman

Garland Publishing, Inc., New York & London

1978

Bibliographical note:

these facsimiles have been made from copies
in the Harvard University Library
Song of the Battle of the Nile (EC8.B6818.799s)
the Bodleian Library of Oxford University
Bowden Hill (280.d.5b9);
The University of Texas Library
The Sorrows of Switzerland (Wn.B681.801s)
The Picture (Wn.B681.803p);
and the Beinecke Library of Yale University
Hope (Mis. Poems 64)
St. Michael's Mount (In.B681.798s)
The Grave of the Last Saxon (In.B681.822)
Ellen Gray (In.B681.823E).

828
B787h

The volumes in this series have been printed on
acid-free, 250-year-life paper.

The title listed in our prospectus as *St. Michael's
Mount,* Salisbury, 1798, and so listed in the Na-
tional Union Catalogue, is a ghost and is identi-
cal with *St. Michael's Mount,* Salisbury, Shaftes-
bury, & London, 1798.

Library of Congress Cataloging in Publication Data
Bowles, William Lisle, 1762-1850.
  Hope, an allegorical sketch.

  (Romantic context : Poetry)
  Reprint of poems published 1796-1823.
  I. Title: Hope, an allegorical sketch.
II. Series.
PR4161.B4A6 1978d   821'.6   75-31166
ISBN 0-8240-2119-3

82-718
Printed in the United States of America

Introduction

Of William Lisle Bowles (1762-1850), Coleridge writes in the first chapter of *Biographia Literaria* (1817): "I had just entered on my seventeenth year, when the sonnets of Mr. Bowles, twenty in number, and just then published in a quarto pamphlet, were first made known and presented to me, by a school-fellow. . . . Dr. Middleton. . . ." He goes on to recollect, with "double pleasure,"

> that I should have received from a friend so revered the first knowledge of a poet, by whose works, year after year, I was so enthusiastically delighted and inspired. . . . As my school finances did not permit me to purchase copies, I made, within less than a year and an half, more than forty transcriptions, as the best present I could offer to those, who had in any way won my regard. And with almost equal delight did I receive the three or four following publications of the same author [I, 13-15]

A few pages later, after tracing particular benefits he received from the subjects and sentiment of Bowles's poems, he writes:

> The reader must make himself acquainted with the general style of composition that was at that time deemed poetry, in order to understand and account for the effect produced on me by the SONNETS, the MONODY at MATLOCK, and the HOPE, of Mr. Bowles; for it is peculiar to original genius to become less and less *striking*, in proportion to its success in improving the taste and judgement of its contemporaries. . . . Bowles and Cowper were, to the best of my knowledge, the first who

INTRODUCTION

combined natural thought with natural diction; the first
who reconciled the heart with the head. [I, 24-25]

Granting what Coleridge says about the change in poetic
idiom between 1789 and 1817 and allowing for the personal
affection he felt for Bowles, who had befriended him during
his stay at Calne, Wiltshire, in 1815-1816, it is fair, I believe, to
say that never has an inferior poetic talent been so egregiously
overpraised by a poetic genius in his years of mature judgment.
As the attentive reader of these volumes will discover, such
praise of Bowles's early poems for combining "natural thought
with natural diction" raises to new heights either sycophancy
or wishful thinking; the entire section on Bowles threatens to
discredit Coleridge's reputation as a practical critic in the very
work on which his claim to such recognition chiefly rests.

William Lisle Bowles was the son of William Thomas
Bowles, a clergyman (whose father and grandfather had also
been clergymen), and of a mother whose father had also been a
clergyman of the established church. After spending his early
years at King's Sutton, Northamptonshire, and then at Uphill,
Somerset, Bowles attended grammar school at Shaftesbury
before going on to Winchester College (1775-1781), where he
came under the influence of Joseph Warton, the headmaster,
and won a prize for Latin prose composition. In 1781 he
proceeded to Trinity College, Oxford, where Warton's brother
Thomas was a senior fellow. In 1782 Bowles was elected to a
scholarship that continued until 1787; at Trinity he also held
another remunerative title and won the chancellor's prize for
Latin verse with a poem on the subject of "The Siege of
Gibraltar." Bowles's father died in 1786. In 1787 he took his
A.B. (M.A., 1792).

Sometime between 1785 and 1788, Bowles became engaged
to a niece of Sir Samuel Romilly. About 1788 she broke off the
engagement at the behest of her parents, who thought
Bowles's professional opportunities too uncertain. Bowles

INTRODUCTION

then undertook a series of tours with the son of an Irish earl, visiting Northern England, Scotland, Belgium, the Rhineland, and Switzerland and recording his impressions in a group of irregular sonnets. Garland Greever, to whose *A Wiltshire Parson and His Friends: The Correspondence of William Lisle Bowles* (1926) I am indebted for most of the facts of this biographical sketch, says that Bowles published his *Fourteen Sonnets* "in an hour of financial need" and recounts how the first edition of 100 copies was followed in the same year (1789) by a 500-copy printing of the enlarged second edition of twenty-one sonnets (obviously the edition which impressed Coleridge so much) and by a total of nine editions through 1805. Sadly, Greever adds, "not only did Bowles fail to produce anything else so good as the sonnets; he never again attracted the same attention by anything he wrote, except indeed in his various pamphlets against Pope" (p. 6).

Instant disillusionment awaits the scholar-critic who turns to Bowles's sonnets immediately after reading Coleridge's encomium and Greever's elegy. For the sonnets, whether taken in the selective first edition or the expanded second, embody almost every variety of sentimentality, faulty diction, awkwardly inverted word order, overobvious alliteration, and corrupted formal structure that has ever been attributed to later eighteenth-century poetry, and they have the additional weakness of the author's failure to spell correctly some of the common words he employs (e.g., "crouded" in Sonnet II of the first edition; see also "ought" used for "aught" three times on page 5 of *Verses to John Howard* [1789]). To understand Coleridge's *early* enthusiasm for Bowles's sonnets (there can be no *logical* reason for his later praise of them), we must forget about conceptions such as "natural thought with natural diction" and center our attention on the subject matter and the themes of Bowles's verse. In his poems over a thirty-year period we not only encounter almost every subject and sentiment contained in the poetry of his younger but greater

INTRODUCTION

contemporaries, but we also find them appearing in about the same order and close to the same chronology in which Coleridge, for example, expressed parallel thoughts on similar topics.

First there was the series of topographical sonnets, filled with melancholy reflections on isolation from home and old friends and on the brevity of human life, interspersed with sentimental praise of the philanthropic endeavors of others (such as the rescue station for shipwrecked sailors at Bamborough Castle) and pious musings on the divine call of the poet himself to higher duties. These themes are echoed and amplified in the poems that follow on John Howard, the universally admired crusader for prison reform, and the *Verses* on the founding of a "Philanthropic Society" to rear and educate the "Children of Vagrants and Criminals" (the kind of scheme viewed more harshly by writers such as Blake, Crabbe, and Dickens who witnessed the results to the children—not just the self-congratulations of the noble institutors). The melancholy muse, thoroughly coached by Thomas Gray, returns in both *Elegy written at the Hot-Wells* and *Monody written at Matlock* (which Coleridge doubtless appreciated especially because the sentiment is directed toward the River Derwent and other scenes dear to him) and recurs periodically—often with a generous portion of self-concern— in poems such as *Elegiac Stanzas, written during Sickness at Bath*. (Greever asserts that Bowles "was one of the greatest cowards, physically, that ever drew breath" [p. 10] and gives several examples of his extraordinary precautions to avoid danger.)

When Bowles turned to poetic subjects of a more public nature—Edmund Burke's writings, the Battle of the Nile, or the subjugation of Switzerland—he again combined humanitarian emphases with a patriotic valuing of England and great Englishmen and detestation of the French that parallel Coleridge's own sentiments by the date of "France: An Ode'

INTRODUCTION

(1798). Add to these affinities the almost lifelong friendship between Coleridge and Bowles, including Bowles's courteous hospitality to Coleridge at one of the darkest moments in STC's life, and the first chapter of *Biographia Literaria* is explained if not totally exculpated.

In 1788 Bowles was appointed curate of Knoyle, Wiltshire, under Dr. Charles Wake, also a prebendary at Westminster. Bowles was engaged in 1792 to Wake's daughter Harriet, but after Dr. Wake tried to break off the match (presumably to arrange a better one), Harriet died in the spring of 1793. In 1797 Bowles married Harriet Wake's younger sister Magdalen. During the early years as curate of Knoyle, Bowles lived at Donhead St. Mary, near Shaftesbury, Dorsetshire, and also very near Fern House, Wilts., the seat of Shelley's maternal uncle Thomas Grove, whose daughter Harriet was Shelley's first fiancée. (See K.N. Cameron, ed., *Shelley and his Circle*, II [1961], 475 ff., especially the map on page 503; there is an unnoted allusion to W.L. Bowles in Harriet Grove's diary on October 9, 1810 [p. 591].) Thus it happened that Bowles visited Thomas Grove's estate at Coombe Ellen in Wales and recorded his feelings in a topographical poem there, as the youthful Shelley was to do a decade later. In 1804 Bowles was appointed vicar of Bremhill near Calne, Wilts., by virtue of an obligation that John Moore, the failing Archbishop of Canterbury (d. 1805), owed to Bowles's maternal grandfather. (Greever tells amusingly how Bowles rushed to Lambeth Palace on the death of the previous incumbent to remind Moore of his promise by repeating over and over "Biddy Grey," the maiden name of Bowles's mother [p. 7].) In 1828 he added the post of Canon Resident at Salisbury Cathedral.

At Bremhill, Bowles had many friends and neighbors, including (eventually) Thomas Moore, George Crabbe, and the third Marquess of Lansdowne, whose country seat, Bowood, was the center of much intellectual and social life—particularly among adherents of the old Whig Connexion. Thus, through

INTRODUCTION

visits to London, socializing at Bowood, and entertaining at his own comfortable vicarage, Bowles managed to meet and cultivate many of the leading writers and intellectual politicians of his day. The true measure of the man seems to be reflected, on the one hand, in his lasting friendships with such people and, on the other, in the record of how they thought of him—as cowardly, naive and credulous, excessively absent-minded (he once put two silk stockings on one leg and then hunted in vain for his second stocking; on another occasion he dismounted and led his horse to a turnpike gate only to discover that the horse had slipped out and left him holding an empty bridle), religiously intolerant, and harsh in judging the motives of those who disagreed with him (see Greever, pp. 9-11). To Greever's list of limitations, I must add that Bowles was a very poor judge of poetry—not only Pope's but his own, which he insisted on publishing and republishing in profusion wihout any apparent awareness (like that which struck Moore, Hunt, and other secondary poets) that his work had far less intrinsic merit than its notoriety would imply.

Having inherited considerable property (which he managed wisely) and enjoying a lucrative ecclesiastical living, Bowles was able to publish almost every word he wrote, much of it at his own expense. The voluminous bibliography of his poetry, sermons, political tracts, and expository prose recorded by Cecil Woolf in *The Book Collector* (VII [1958], 286-294; 407-416) has recently been supplemented by Geoffrey Little and Elizabeth Hall in the same journal (XXVI [1977]). The whole range of his publications exhibits a lack of taste and self-critical discrimination that—encouraged by excessive praise from friends such as Coleridge and Southey—resulted in a disabling literary vanity. This weakness shows itself to disastrous effect in his attack on Pope in *The Invariable Principles of Poetry* (1819) and subsequent critical tracts through 1826, in which his two chief antagonists were Thomas Campbell and Lord Byron. The episode—though it did not elevate Byron's contemporary

INTRODUCTION

reputation—left Bowles marked for posterity as the equal of one of Dryden's Grub Street antagonists or one of Pope's dunces, as had the derogatory lines by Hobhouse (q.v.) and Byron in the various editions of *English Bards and Scotch Reviewers.*

Thomas Moore knew Bowles well and generally liked him; in February 1818, both in a letter to Rogers and in his journal, he remarked that "it is not of Helicon that his spirit has drunk," but "at least of very sweet waters, and to my taste very delightful" (Moore, *Letters,* ed. W.S. Dowden, I, 442). But elsewhere in his journal (February 1, 1819) he writes: "Received a note from Bowles, in which he said, 'Have you seen the *"Quarterly"*? they are very complimentary to me as an author.' How lucky it is that self-love has always something comfortable to retire upon!" Moore was referring to the generally hostile tone of the *Quarterly* and other reviewers that left Bowles very little food for his self-esteem but that nourished it anyway.

Though it may be asked why, if Bowles is such an incompetent poet, critic, and thinker, he occupies a substantial place in the Romantic Context, I can answer only that literary history (like political history) repeatedly plays similar strange tricks with merit and mediocrity. And yet it would be a slander on the period to imply that Bowles received widespread acclaim. Enthusiasm for his poetry was largely confined to the circles of his two most vocal admirers, Coleridge and Southey, during the 1790s. Lamb, for example, who quotes and praises Bowles (along with Burns and Cowper, whom he admired more) in letters to Coleridge through 1797, writes to Robert Lloyd on November 13, 1798, of "the race of sonnet writers & complainers, Bowless & Charlotte Smiths, & all that tribe, who can see no joys but what are past, and fill peoples' heads with notions of the Unsatisfying nature of Earthly comforts" (Lamb, *Letters,* ed. E.W. Marrs, I, 144), thereafter entirely dropping mention of Bowles's poetry from his correspon-

INTRODUCTION

dence. Landor, who knew Bowles, never discusses him as a literary figure. Hazlitt ignores Bowles in his *Lectures on the English Poets* and mentions him in *The Spirit of the Age* only as a passing enthusiasm of Coleridge and as the controversial adversary of Byron (the latter role also occasioning Shelley's single reference to Bowles). Wordsworth purchased and read with some enthusiasm Bowles's *Fourteen Sonnets* in 1789 (see Mary Moorman, *William Wordsworth*, I, 124-125); his interest in Bowles must have been nurtured by his later associations with Coleridge. Yet Wordsworth never in his letters, prose, or recorded conversations speaks of Bowles as a significant or even interesting poet, and it seems likely that any influence Bowles may have had on Wordsworth's earliest sonnets was soon rejected in favor of Milton and other models.

There is, perhaps, a natural level that mature literary figures find at which they compare themselves with those of similar stature—attempting to emulate or to excel them. In this regard it is interesting to note that whereas Keats never condescends to mention Bowles, John Hamilton Reynolds in a paper for *The Champion*, April 7, 1816, entitled "The Pilgrimage of Living Poets to the Stream of Castaly," compares Bowles and a handful of other poetasters to "a flock of geese wash[ing] themselves in a pond with gabbling importance." Bowles, who was sent the offending issue of *The Champion* by "a good natured friend," rose to the bait and sent the weekly a self-congratulatory reply that more than justified Reynolds' characterization (see Reynolds, *Selected Prose*, ed. L.M. Jones, pp. 50-52). The exchange is instructive. As Hobhouse rather than Byron composed the attack on Bowles included in the first edition of *English Bards and Scotch Reviewers* and as Byron—aside from substituting his own lines in later editions to make the poem entirely his own—virtually ignored Bowles as a poet until Bowles attacked Pope, so Keats, a poet of the first rank, does not even think of Bowles, while Reynolds, himself a poet of the third rank, sets out to attack him. The moral carries over

INTRODUCTION

to praise as well as to blame, for third-rate writers are always discovering other third-rate writers, either forerunners or contemporaries, who are "unjustly neglected" by the critics.

One purely technical and mechanical use to which scholars will be able to put these reprints of Bowles's early editions is to observe the possible pronunciations of certain common words current under the poetic license of the Romantic period, for Bowles indicates the omission of syllables from optionally pronounced words by means of replacing the silent vowel with an apostrophe. Since he had control of the printing and gave attention to such minutiae, his works are more carefully consistent in this regard than the works of his greater contemporaries, who followed the practice less inflexibly.

Donald H. Reiman

H O P E,

AN ALLEGORICAL SKETCH,

ON

RECOVERING SLOWLY FROM SICKNESS.

BY

THE REVEREND W. L. BOWLES, A.M.

But thou, O Hope, with eyes fo fair,
What was thy delighted meafure?
Still it whifper'd promis'd pleafure,
And bid the lovely fcenes at diftance hail.
COLLINS.

LONDON:

PRINTED FOR DILLY, IN THE POULTRY; CADELL & DAVIES, IN THE STRAND; AND CRUTTWELL, AT BATH.

MDCCXCVI.

TO THE MOST REVEREND

WILLIAM,

ARCHBISHOP OF YORK,

IN GRATITUDE FOR KINDNESS AND CIVILITIES

EXPERIENCED FROM HIM

DURING SICKNESS,

AND

WITH SINCERE PRAYERS

FOR THE PERFECT ESTABLISHMENT OF

HIS HEALTH,

THESE STANZAS

ARE RESPECTFULLY INSCRIBED,

BY HIS MOST OBEDIENT SERVANT,

THE AUTHOR.

DONHEAD, *Auguft* 10, 1796.

ADVERTISEMENT.

THE Author takes this opportunity of expreſſing his regret that the Second Edition of his prior little Poem (written in ſickneſs) ſhould have appeared, before he could avail himſelf of the judicious ſuggeſtions of the Critical Review reſpecting the ſtrict ſenſe of the word Contentment.

He will always be happy to pay attention to obſervations which are conveyed in the language of candour and liberality.

It need not be added that the primary idea of this ſketch was taken from the exquiſite picture by COLLINS, in his Ode on the Paſſions. The deſcriptive part was ſuggeſted by the ſcenery on the banks of the Southampton River, where the Author occaſionally took his morning walks in the beginning of May, after tedious and melancholy confinement.

HOPE,

AN ALLEGORICAL SKETCH.

I.

" I Am the comforter of thofe that mourn,
  " My fcenes well-fhadow'd, and my carol fweet,
" Cheer the poor paffengers of life's rude bourne,
  " Till they are fhelter'd in that laft retreat,
" Where human toils and troubles are forgot."
  Thefe founds I heard amid this mortal road,
When I had reach'd with pain one pleafant fpot,
  So that for joy fome tears in filence flow'd;
I rais'd mine eyes, which ficknefs long depreft,
And felt thy warmth, O fun, come cheering to my breaft.

II.

The ſtorm of night had ceas'd upon the plain,
　　When thoughtful in the foreſt-walk I ſtray'd,
To the long hollow murmur of the main
　　Liſt'ning, and to the many leaves that made
A drowſy cadence, as the high trees wav'd;
When ſtraight a beauteous ſcene burſt on my ſight;
　　Smooth were the waters that the low-land lav'd;
And lo! a form, as of ſome fairy ſprite,
That held in her right-hand a budding ſpray,*
And like a ſea-maid ſung her ſweetly-warbled lay.

III.

Soothing as ſteals the ſummer-wave ſhe ſung,
　" The griſly phantoms of the night are gone
　" To hear in ſhades forlorn the death-bell rung;
　　" But thou whom ſickneſs has left weak and wan

---

* The Ancients repreſented Hope with a bud, juſt opening, in her hand.
See SPENCE's Polymetis.

" Turn from their fpe&tre-terrors; the green fea
  " That whifpers at my feet, the matin gale
 ' That crifps its fhining marge, *fhall folace thee,
   " And thou my long-forgotten voice fhalt hail,
" For I am Hope, whom weary hearts confefs
" The footheft fprite that fings on life's long wildernefs."

IV.

As flowly ceas'd her tender voice, I ftood,
    Delighted: the hard way fo lately paft,
Seem'd fmooth; the ocean's bright-extended flood
    Before me ftretch'd; the clouds that overcaft
Heaven's melancholy vault, hurried away,
    Driv'n feaward, and the azure hills appear'd;
The fun-beams fhone upon their fummits grey,
    Strange faddening founds no more by fits were heard,
But birds, † in new leaves fhrouded, fung aloft,
And o'er the level feas fpring's healing airs blew foft.

---

* Isaac Walton's Song in the Complete Fifherman.
        I in thefe flow'ry meads would be,
        Thefe cryftal ftreams *fhould folace me.*

† Foliis adoperta novellis.   Milton, Eleg.
        B

V.

As when a traveller, who, many days
    Hath journey'd 'mid Arabian deferts ftill,
A dreary folitude far on furveys,
    Nor hears, or flitting bird, or gufhing rill,
But near fome marble ruin, gleaming pale,
    Sighs, mindful of the haunts of cheerful man,
And thinks he hears in every fickly gale
    The bells of fome flow-wheeling caravan ·
At length, emerging o'er the dim tract, fees
Gay domes, and golden fanes, and minarets, and trees:

VI.

So beat my bofom when my winding way
    Led thro' the thickets to a fhelter'd vale,
Where the fweet minftrel fat: a fmooth clear bay
    Skirted with woods appear'd, where many a fail,
Went fhining o'er the watery furface ftill,
    Leff'ning at laft in the grey ocean-flood;
And yonder, half-way up the fronting hill,
    Peeping from forth the trees, a cottage ftood,
Above whofe peaceful umbrage, trailing high,
A little fmoke went up, and ftain'd the cloudlefs fky.

VII.

I turn'd, and lo, a mountain feem'd to rife,
  Upon whofe top a fpiry citadel
Lifted its dim-feen turrets to the fkies,
  Where fome high lord of the domain might dwell :
And onward where the eye fcarce ftretch'd its fight,
  Hills over hills in long fucceffion rofe,
Touch'd with a fofter and yet fofter light,
  And all was blended as in deep repofe,
The wood, the fea, the hills that fhone fo fair,
Till woods, and fea, and hills feem'd fading into air.

VIII.

At once, methought, I faw a various throng
  To this enchanting fpot their footfteps bend,
All drawn, fweet Hope, by thy infpiring fong,
  Which melodies fcarce mortal feem'd to blend.
Firft buxom Youth, with cheeks of glowing red,
  Came lightly tripping o'er the morning dew,
He wore a hare-bell garland on his head,
  And ftretch'd his hands at the bright-burfting view :
A mountain fawn went bounding by his fide,
Around whofe flender neck a filver bell was tied.

[6]

IX.

Then faid I, Miftrefs of the magic fong,

    O pity 'twere that hearts which know no guile

Should ever feel the pangs of ruth or wrong!

    She heeded not, but fung with lovelier fmile,

" Enjoy, O youth, the feafon of thy May,

    " Hark, how the throftles in the hawthorn fing,

" The hoary time, * that refteth night nor day,

    " O'er the earth's fhade may fpeed with noifelefs wing;

" But heed not thou: fnatch the brief joys that rife,

" † And fport beneath the light of thefe unclouded fkies."

---

* See CHAUCER's Romance of the Rofe.

> The time, that paffeth night and day,
> And reftleffe travaileth aye,
> And fteleth from us fo prively
> That to us feemeth fykerly
> That it in one point dwelleth ever,
> And certes it ne refteth never.

† The reader will recollect Mrs. Smith's affecting and moft beautiful Sonnet,

" Sorrowing I fee yon little tribe at play."

X.

His fine eye flafhing an unwonted fire,
　　Then Fancy o'er the glade delighted went;
He ftruck at times a fmall and filver lyre,
　　Or gaz'd upon the rolling element;
Sometimes he took his mirror which did fhow
　　The various landfcape lovelier than the life;
More beamy bright the vivid tints did glow,
　　And fo well mingled was the color's ftrife
That the fond heart, the beauteous fhades once feen,
Would figh for fuch retreats, for vales and woods fo green!

XI.

Gay was his afpect, and his airy veft,
　　As loofe it flow'd, fuch colors did difplay,
As paint the clouds repofing in the weft,
　　Or the moift rainbow's radiant arch inlay;
And now he tripp'd, like fairy of the wood,
　　And feem'd with dancing fpirits to rejoice,
And now he hung his head in penfive mood—
　　Meantime, O Hope, he liften'd to thy voice,
And whilft of joy and youth it cheerly fung,
Lightly he touch'd his harp, and o'er the valley fprung.

XII.

Beauty, a gay coquette, to the glad found
   Danc'd, as her heart was all on pleasures set,
And now she gaz'd with a sweet archness round,
   And wantonly display'd a silken net:
She won her way with fascinating air—.
   Her eyes illumin'd with a tender light,
Her smile's strange blandishment, her shaded hair
   That length'ning hung, her teeth like ivory white,
That peep'd from her moist lip, seem'd to inspire
Tumultuous wishes warm, and dreams of fond desire.

XIII.

What softer passions did thy bosom move,
   When those melodious measures met thine ear,
Child of sincerity, and virtuous love?
   Thine eyes did shine beneath a blissful tear
That still were turned to the tranquil scene,
   Where the thin smoke rose from th'embow'red cot;
And thou didst think, that there, with smile serene,
   In quiet shades, and every pang forgot,
Thou mightest sink on pure Affection's breast,
And listen to the winds that whisper'd thee to rest.

XIV.

I thought, " O Love, how feldom art thou found

    " Without annoyance in this earthly ftate !

  " * For haply thou doft feed fome rankling wound,

    " Or on thy youth pale poverty doth wait,

  " Till years on years heavy are roll'd away;

    " Or where thou moft didft hope firm faith to fee,

  " Thou meeteft ficklenefs eftrang'd and cold ;

    " Or if fome true and tender heart there be

" On which, through every change, thy foul might truft,

" Death comes with his fell dart, and fmites it to the duft."

XV.

But lufty Enterprize, with looks of glee

    Approach'd the drooping youth, as he would fay,

  " Come to the high woods, and the hills with me,

    " And caft thy fullen myrtle-wreath away !"

---

* Midfummer Night's Dream,

       Hermia, for aught that ever I could read,

       Could ever hear by tale or hiftory,

       The courfe of true love never did run fmcoth,

       But either it was different in blood,

       Or elfe mifgraffed in refpect of years,

       Or elfe it ftood upon the choice of friends,

       Or if there were a fympathy in choice,

       War, death, or ficknefs, did lay fiege to it.

Upon a neighing courſer he did ſit,

    That ſtretch'd its arched neck, in conſcious pride,

And champ'd as with diſdain its golden bit,

    But Hope her animating * voice applied,

And Enterprize with ſpeed impetuous paſs'd,

Whilſt the long vale return'd his wreathed bugle's blaſt.

XVI.

Suddenly, lifting high his pond'rous ſpear,

    A mailed man came forth with ſcornful pride,

I ſaw him tow'ring in his dark career

    Along the valley like a giant ſtride:

Upon his helm, in letters of bright gold,

    That to the ſun's meridian ſplendor ſhone,

Ambition's name far off I might behold.

    Meantime from earth there came a hollow moan :

But Fame, who follow'd, her loud trumpet blew,

And to the murmuring beach with eyes on flame he flew.

---

    * Dejeſted Pity at his ſide,
      Her ſoul-ſubduing *voice applied*.
                COLLINS.

XVII.

And now already had he gain'd the ſtrand,

    Where a tall veſſel rode with ſail unfurl'd,

And ſoon he thought to reach the farther land,

    Which to his eager eye ſeem'd like a world

That he by ſtrength might win and make his own,

    And in that citadel, which ſhone ſo bright,

Seat him, a purple ſovereign, on his throne.

    So he went tilting o'er the waters white,

And whilſt he oft look'd back with ſtern diſdain,

In louder tones, methought, was heard the inſpiring ſtrain.

XVIII.

" By the ſhade of cities old,

    " By many a river ſtain'd with gore,

" By the ſword of * Seſac bold

    " Who ſmote the nations from the ſhore

---

* Seſac, Bacchus, or Seſoſtris (according to Sir Iſaac Newton) one and the ſame king of Ægypt, who conquered weſtward as far as the Pillars of Hercules, and eaſtward to the Ganges. He ſet up two pillars in India, on the mountains, near the mouth of the Ganges.

C

" Of ancient Nile to India's fartheft plain,

　" By Fame's proud pillars, and by Valour's fhield,

" By mighty chiefs in glorious battle flain,

　" Affert thy fway : amid the bloody field

" Purfue thy march, and to the heights fublime

" Of Honor's glittering cliffs, a mighty conqueror, climb.

XIX.

Then faid I in mine heart, " Man, thou doft rear

　" Thine eye to Heav'n, and vaunt thy lofty worth :

" The enfign of dominion thou doft bear

　" O'er nature's works ; but thou doft oft go forth,

" Urg'd by falfe hopes, to ravage and deftroy ;

　" Thou doft build up a name by cruel deeds,

" Whilft to the peaceful fcenes of love and joy,

　" Sorrow, and Crime, and Solitude fucceeds.

" Hence, when her war-fong Victory doth fing,

" Deftruction flaps aloft her iron-hurtling wing."

XX.

But fee, as one awak'd from deadly trance,
 With hollow and dim eyes and ftony ftare,
Captivity with faltering ftep advance !
 Dripping and knotted was her coal-black hair :
For fhe had long been hid, as in the grave ;
 No founds the filence of her prifon broke,
Nor one companion had fhe in her cave
 Save Terror's difmal fhape, that no word fpoke,
But to a ftony coffin on the floor
With lean and hideous finger pointed evermore.

XXI.

The lark's fhrill fong, the early village chime,
 The upland echo of the winding horn,
The far-heard clock that fpoke the paffing time,
 Had never pierc'd her folitude forlorn :
At length releas'd from the deep dungeon's gloom
 She feels the fragrance of the vernal gale,
She fees more fweet the living landfcape bloom,
 And whilft fhe liftens to Hope's tender tale,
She thinks her long-loft friends fhall blefs her fight,
And almoft faints with joy amidft the broad day-light.

XXII.

And near the fpot, as with reluctant feet,
  Slowly defponding Melancholy drew,
The wind and rain her naked breaft had beat,
  Sunk was her eye, and fallow was her hue.
In the huge foreft's unrejoicing fhade
  Bewilder'd had fhe wander'd day by day,
And many a grifly fiend her heart difmay'd,
  And cold and wet upon the ground fhe lay,
But now fuch founds with mellow fweetnefs ftole,
As lapp'd in dreams of blifs her flow-confenting foul.

XXIII.

Next to the gleamy glen, poor Mania ftray'd:
  Moft pale and wild, yet gentle was her look,
A flender garland fhe of ftraw had made,
  Of flow'rs, and rufhes from the running brook;
But as fhe fadly pafs'd, the tender found
  Of its fharp pang her wounded heart beguil'd,
She dropp'd her half-made garland on the ground,
  And then fhe figh'd, and then in tears fhe fmil'd,
But fmiled fo, that Pity would have faid,
" O God be merciful to that poor haplefs maid!"

XXIV.

Now ravingly fhe cried, " The whelming main,
  " The wintry wave rolls over his cold head,
" I never fhall behold my love again—
  " Hence, flattering fancies—he is dead, is dead !
" Perhaps upon fome wild fhore he is caft,
  " Where on their prey Barbarians howling rufh,
" O fiercer they, than is the whelming blaft !
  " Hufh, my poor heart,—my wakeful forrows, hufh !
" He lives—I yet fhall prefs him to my heart,
" And cry, O no, no, no,—we never more will part !"

XXV.

So fung fhe, when defpairing from his cell,
  Hid fartheft in the lone umbrageous wood,
Where many a winter he had lov'd to dwell,
  Came grim Remorfe : as fixt in thought he ftood,
His fenfes pierc'd by the unwonted tone
  He heard—the blood-drops from his locks he fhook—
He faw the trees that wav'd, the fun that fhone,
  He caft around an agonized look ;
Then with a ghaftly fmile that fpoke his pain,
He hied him to his cave in thickeft fhades again.

XXVI.

And now the fun funk weftward, and the fky
    Was hung with thoufand lucid pictures gay;
When gazing on the fcene with placid eye,
    An ancient man appear'd in amice grey.
His fandal fhoes were by long travel worn,
    O'er hill and valley, many a ling'ring mile,
Yet droop'd he not, like one in years forlorn;
    His pale cheek wore a fad, but tender, fmile;
'Twas fage Experience, by his look confefs'd,
And white as froft his beard defcended to his breaft.

XXVII.

* Then faid I, Mafter, pleafant is this place,
    And fweet are thofe melodious notes I hear,
And happy they among man's toiling race
    Who, of their cares forgetful, wander near:
Me they delight whom ficknefs and flow pain,
    Have bow'd almoft to death with heavy hand,
The fairy fcenes refrefh my heart again,
    And pleas'd I liften to that mufic bland,

---

* Ed Io, Mæftro, &c.   DANTE, Inferno.

Which feems to promife hours of joy to come,
And bids me tranquil feek my poor but peaceful home.

XXVIII.

He faid, " Alas thefe fhadows foon may fly,
  " Like the gay landfcapes of the element :
" Yet do poor mortals ftill with raptur'd eye,
  " Behold like thee the pictures they prefent ;
" And charm'd by Hope's fweet mufic on they fare,
  " And think they foon fhall reach that blifsful goal
" Where never more the fullen knell of Care
  " Departed friends and fever'd loves fhall toll :
" So on they fare ; till all their troubles ceafe,
" And on a lap of earth they lay them down in peace.

XXIX.

" But not there ceafes their immortal claim
  " (From golden clouds I heard a fmall voice fay),
" Wifdom rejoiceth in a higher aim,
  " Nor heeds the tranfient fhadows of a day.

" Thefe earthly founds may die away, and all

    " Thefe perifhable pictures fink in night,

" But Virtue from the duft her fons fhall call,

    " And lead them forth to joy, and life, and light,

" Tho' from their languid grafp earth's comforts fly,

" And with the filent worm their buried bodies lie.

XXX.

" For other fcenes there are, and in a clime

    " Purer, and other ftrains to earth unknown,

" Where Heaven's high hoft with fymphonies fublime

    " Sing " Unto Him that fitteth on the throne."

" Enough for man if he the tafk fulfil

    " Which GOD ordain'd, and to his journey's end

" Bear him right on, betide him good or ill;

    " Then Hope to foothe his death-bed fhall defcend,

" * Nor leave him, till in manfions of the bleft

" He gain his deftin'd home, his everlafting reft."

---

* Nor leaves us till we die.   POPE.

THE END.

ST. MICHAEL'S MOUNT,

A POEM.

BY

THE REV. WILLIAM LISLE BOWLES.

SALISBURY:

PRINTED BY B. C. COLLINS, FOR T. ADAMS, SHAFTESBURY; AND SOLD BY DILLY,
LONDON, AND ALL OTHER BOOKSELLERS.

1798.

TO

THE RIGHT HON. LORD SOMMERS,

BARON OF EVESHAM,

THIS

𝕾mall 𝕻oem

IS RESPECTFULLY INSCRIBED,

BY

HIS MUCH OBLIGED AND OBEDIENT SERVANT,

The Author.

ST. MICHAEL'S MOUNT.

—

A POEM.

—

WHILE Summer airs fcarce breathe along the tide,
Oft paufing, up the Mountain's craggy fide
We climb:—how beautiful, how ftill, how clear,
The fcenes that ftretch around!—the rocks that rear
Their fhapes, in rich fantaftic colours dreft;
The hill-tops, where the fofteft fhadows reft;
The long-retiring bay; the level fand;
The fading fea-line, and the fartheft land
That feems, as faint it leffens from the eye,
To fteal away, beneath the cloudlefs fky!

BUT yefterday, the mifty morn was fpread
In drearinefs on the bleak mountain's head;
No glittering profpect from the upland fmil'd;
The driving fquall came dark, the fea heav'd wild,

B   And

And loſt and lonely, the way-farer ſigh'd,
Wet with the hoar ſpray of the flaſhing tide!
How chang'd is now the circling ſcene! the deep
Stirs not; the glancing roofs and white tow'rs peep
Along the margin of the lucid bay;
The ſails, deſcried far in the offing grey,
Hang motionleſs, and the pale headland's height
Is touch'd as with ſweet gleams of fairy light!

Oh! live there on earth's buſy-ſtirring ſcene
Whom nature's tranquil charms, her airs ſerene,
Her ſeas, her ſkies, her ſun-beams, fail to move
With ſtealing tenderneſs, and grateful love?
Go, thankleſs man, to miſery's cave: behold
Captivity, ſtretch'd in her dungeon cold;
Or think on thoſe, who in yon dreary mine,
* Sunk fathoms deep beneath the rolling brine
From year to year, amid the lurid ſhade,
O'er-wearied, ply their melancholy trade,

* A Mine, called the Wherry-Mine beneath the ſurface of the ſea, near
Penzance.

That

That thou may'ſt bleſs the glorious ſun, and hail
Him, who with beauty cloath'd the hill and vale;
Who bent the arch of the high heav'ns for thee,
And ſtretch'd in amplitude the broad blue ſea.

Now ſunk are all its murmurs! and the air
But moves by fits the bents, that, here and there,
Upſhoot in caſual ſpots of faded green:
Here ſtraggling ſheep the ſcanty paſture glean—
Or, on the jutting fragments that impend,
Stray fearleſsly, and gaze, as we aſcend.

MOUNTAIN!* no pomp of waving woods haſt thou,
That deck with varied ſhade thy hoary brow;
No ſunny meadows at thy feet are ſpread,
No ſtreamlets ſparkle o'er their pebbly bed :

---

* Three or four ſheep were ſeen rambling among the precipices, and
picking here and there a blade of graſs; but in general the Rock, is naked,
and extremely ſteep and craggy.

But

But thou canſt boaſt thy beauties ; ample views
That catch the rapt eye of the pauſing Muſe ;
Headlands around new-lighted ; ſails, and ſeas
Now glaſſy-ſmooth, now wrinkling to the breeze—
And when the driſly Winter, wrapt in ſleet,
Goes by, and winds and rain thy ramparts beat,
Fancy can ſee thee ſtanding thus aloof,
And frowning, bleak, and bare, and tempeſt-proof,
Look down, as in ſtern confidence, and brave
The howling hurricane, the daſhing wave ;
More graceful, when the ſtorm's dark vapours frown,
Than when the ſummer ſuns in all their pomp go down!

AND ſuch is he, who, clad in homely weeds,
And boaſting little more than Nature needs,
Can wrap him in contentedneſs, and wear
A port unchang'd, in ſeaſons rude or fair.
His may be Fancy's ſunſhine ; and the Muſe
May deck his viſions with her faireſt hues,

And

And he may lift his honeſt front, and ſay
To the hard ſtorm, that rends his locks of grey,
" I heed thee not;" He unappall'd may ſtand
Beneath the cloud that ſhades a ſinking land,
(When, heedleſs of the ſtorm that onward ſweeps,
Mad impious Riot his loud waſſal keeps)
Pre-eminent in native worth; nor bend,
Tho' gathering ills on his bare head deſcend:
And when the waſteful ſtorm ſweeps o'er its prey,
And rends the kingdoms of the world away,
He, firm as ſtands the Rock's unſhaken baſe,
Yet panting for a ſurer reſting-place,
The human hurricane unmov'd can ſee,
And ſay, " O God, my refuge is in Thee!"

STATES, anchored deep, that far their ſhadow caſt,
Rock, and are ſcatter'd by the Almighty's blaſt!
As when, awaken'd from his horrid ſleep,
In fiery caves, a thouſand fathoms deep,
The Earthquake's Dæmon hies aloft,—he waits,
Awhile, by ſome renowned city's gates,

As lift'ning to the mingled fhouts and din
Of the mad crowd that feaft or dance within;
Meantime fad Nature feels his fway,—the wave
Heaves, and low founds moan thro' the Mountain cave,
Then all at once is ftill:—ftill as Mid-Night,
When not the lime-leaf moves.—O, piteous fight!
For now the glittering domes crafh from on high—
And hark! a ftrange and lamentable cry—
It ceafes—and the tide's departing roar
Alone is heard upon the defert fhore,
That, as it fweeps, with flow huge fwell, away,
Remorfelefs mutters o'er its buried prey.

So Ruin hurrieth o'er this fhaken ball—
He lifts his mighty mace, and lo! they fall,
A Carthage or a Rome:—then rolls the tide
Of deep Forgetfulnefs, whelming the pride
Of man, his fhatter'd and forfaken bow'rs,
His noifelefs cities, and his proftrate tow'rs!
Some columns, eminent and awful, ftand,
Like Ægypt's pillars on the lonely fand;

We

We read upon their bafe, infcrib'd by Fame,
An Homer's here, or here a Shakefpeare's name,
Yet think not of the furge, that foon may fweep
Ourfelves unnumber'd to th' oblivious Deep.

*THE time has been, as mould'ring legends fay,
When all yon Weftern tract, and this bright bay,
(Where now the funfhine fleeps, and wheeling white
The fea-mew circles in fantaftic flight)
Was peopled wide ; but the loud ftorm hath rav'd
Where its green top the high wood whifpering wav'd,
And many a year the flowly-rifing flood
Rak'd, where the Druids uncouth altar ftood.—
Thou only, aged Mountain ! doft remain,
Stern monument amidft the delug'd plain ;
And fruitlefs the big waves thy bulwarks beat—
The big waves flow retire, and murmur at thy feet† :

* Tradition reports, that the Rock was anciently connected by a large
tract of land with the Ifles of Scilly, and that the whole fpace between was
inundated by an incurfion of the fea.

† It is only at high tide the Rock is entirely furrounded by the fea : at
low-water it is acceffible by land.

THOU,

THOU, half-encircled by the refluent tide,

As if thy ſtate its utmoſt rage defied,

Doſt tow'r above the ſcene as in thine ancient pride. ⎱

MOUNTAIN ! the curious Muſe might love to gaze

On the dim record of thy early days,

Oft fanc'ing that ſhe heard, like the low blaſt,

The ſounds of mighty generations paſt.—

THEE the Phœnician, as remote he ſail'd

Along the unknown coaſt, exulting hail'd,

And when he ſaw thy rocky point aſpire,

Thought on his native ſhores of Aradus or Tyre!

Diſtain'd with many a ghaſtly giant's blood,

Upon thy height huge *Corineus ſtood,

And claſh'd his ſhield ; whilſt, hid in caves profound,

His monſtrous foe cower'd at the fearful ſound.—

Hark to the brazen clarions' pealing ſwell!

The ſhout, at intervals, the deep'ning yell!

---

* One of the ſuppoſed followers of Brutus, to whom Cornwall was allotted ; " The rather by him lik'd," ſays MILTON, " for that the hugeſt giants in rocks and caves were ſaid to lurk there, which kind of monſters to deal with was his old exerciſe."

To

Long ages fpeed away, yet now again
The noife of battle *hurtles on the plain!*
Behold the painted warriors!—down thy fide,
O Mountain! fternly-terrible, they ftride!
E'en now, impatient for the promis'd war,
*They rear their axes huge, and fhouting, cry to Thor!

THE founds of conflict ceafe—at dead of night
A voice is heard, " prepare the Druid rite ;"—
And hark ! the bard upon thy fummit rings
The deep chords of his thrilling harp, and fings
To Night's pale Queen, that thro' the Heavens wide,
Amidft her ftill hoft lift'ning, feems to ride!
Slow finks the cadence of the folemn lay,
And all the fomb'rous fcen'ry fteals away,—
The fhadowy Druid throng, the darkfome wood,
And the hoar altar, wet with human blood.

*. At the bottom of this mountain, as they were digging for tin, they found fpear-heads, axes, &c. (CAMDEN.)

C   MARK'D

Mark'd ye the Angel-fpeƈtre that appear'd?—
By other hands the *holy fane is rear'd,
High on the point, where, gazing o'er the flood,
Confefs'd the glitt'ring Apparition ftood—
And now, far off, upon his watch of night,
The mariner fees the tall window's light,
Or homeward bound, hears on the twilight bay
The flowly-chanted vefpers die away!

These fcenes are fled and pafs'd, yet ftill fublime,
And wearing graceful the grey tints of Time,
Upon the fteep Rock's craggy eminence
Th' embattled Caftle fits, furveying thence
The villages that ftrew the fubjeƈt plain,
And the long winding of the lucid main;
Meantime the ftranger marks its turrets high,
And mufes on the tale of changeful years gone by!

* A convent built on the top of the Rock, where the apparition of St.
Michael was faid to have appeared.

BUT

But truce to fancies—lo ! our travel ends,
Wide and more wide the arch of Heav'n extends,
And on this top-moſt fragment as we lean,
We feel remov'd from dim earth's diſtant ſcene.
Lift up the hollow trump *, that on the ground
Is caſt, and let it, rolling its long ſound,
Speak to the ſurge below, that we may gain
Tidings from thoſe who traverſe the wide main !
Or tread we now ſome ſpot of wizard-land ?
And mark the ſable trump, that may command
The brazen doors to fly, and with loud call
Scare the grim Giant in his murky hall !
Hail, ſolitary Caſtle ! that doſt crown
This deſert ſummit, and ſupreme look down
On the long leſſening landſcape ſtretch'd below;
Fearleſs to trace thy inmoſt haunts we go !

We climb the ſteps :—No warning ſigns are ſent,
No fiery ſhapes flaſh on the battlement !

* A ſpeaking-trumpet lying on the ground.

We

We enter:—the long chambers, without fear,

We traverfe:—No ftrange echoes meet the ear,

No time-worn tapeftry fpontaneous fhakes,

No fpell-bound maiden from her trance awakes,

But Tafte's fair hand arrays the peaceful dome—

And hither the domeftic virtues come,

Pleas'd, while to this fecluded fcene* they bear

Sweets that oft wither in a world of care.

CASTLE, no more thou frowneft on the main

In the dark terror of thy ancient reign;

No more thy long and dreary halls affright,

Swept by the ftoled fpirits of the night ;

But calm, and heedlefs of the ftorms that beat,

Here Elegance and Peace affume their feat;

And when the Night defcends, and Ocean roars,

Rocking without upon his darken'd fhores,

* The Caftle, which belongs to Sir John St. Aubyn, was tenanted by Sir
Walter James and Lady.

Thefe

These vaulted roofs to gentle founds reply
The voice of focial cheer, or fong of harmony.*

So fade the modes of life with flow decay,
And various ages various hues difplay!
Fled are the grimly fhadows of Romance,
And pleas'd we fee in beauteous troop advance
New arts, new manners, from the gothic gloom
Efcap'd, and fcattering flow'rs that fweetlier bloom!

REFINEMENT wakes—before her beaming eye
Difpers'd, the fumes of feudal darknefs fly.
Like orient morning on the Mountain's head,
A fofter light on life's wide fcene is fhed:
Lapping in blifs the fenfe of human cares,
MELODY pours forth her ten thoufand airs;
And, like the fhades that on the ftill lake lye,
Of rocks, or fringing woods, or tinted fky,

* This, and the foregoing reflections, were fuggefted by feeing inftru-
ments of mufic, books, &c. in an apartment, elegantly, but appropriately
fitted up.

PAINTING

PAINTING her hues on the clear tablet lays,
And her own beauteous world with tender touch difplays!
Then SCIENCE lifts her form, auguft and fair,
And fhakes the night-dews from her glitt'ring hair:
Meantime rich CULTURE cloaths the living wafte,
And purer patterns of ATHENIAN TASTE
Invite the eye, and wake the kindling fenfe;
And milder MANNERS, as they play, difpenfe,
Like tepid airs of Spring, their genial influence.

SUCH is thy boaft, REFINEMENT; but deep dies
Oft mar the fplendor of thy noon-tide fkies:
Then Fancy, fick of follies that deform
The face of day, and in the funfhine fwarm;
Sick of the fluttering fopp'ries that engage
The vain purfuits of a degenerate age;
Sick of fmooth Sophiftry's infidious cant,
Or cold Impiety's defying rant;
Sick of the muling fentiment that fighs
O'er its dead bird, while Want unpitied cries;

Sick

Sick of the pictures that pale Luft inflame,
And flufh the cheek of Love with deep deep fhame;
Would fain the fhade of elder days recall,
The gothic battlements, the banner'd hall,
Or lift of Elfin harps the fabling rhyme,
Or wrapt in melancholy trance fublime,
Paufe o'er the working of fome wond'rous tale,
Or bid the Spectres of the Caftle hail!—

O MIGHT I now, amid the frowning ftorm,
Behold, great Vifion of the Mount, thy form,
Such and fo vaft as thou wert feen of yore,
When, looking ftedfaft to Bayona's fhore,
Thou fatteft awful on the topmoft ftone,
Making the Rock thy folitary throne!
For up the narrow fteps, winding with pain,
The watch-tow'r's loftieft platform now we gain:
Departed fpirit, fruitlefs is the pray'r,
We fee alone thy long deferted chair,*

* On the higheft turret of the Caftle is a place which is called "St. Michael's Chair."

And

And never more, or in the ſtorm of night,
Or by the glimm'ring Moon's illuſive light,
Or when the flaſh, with red and haſty glance,
Sudden illumes the ſea's remote expanſe,
The ſhores, the cliffs, the mountain, (till again
Deep darkneſs cloſes on the roaring main)
Shalt thou, dread Angel, with unalter'd mein,
Sublime upon thy cloudy ſeat be ſeen!

Yet, muſing much on wild tradition's lore,
And many a phantom tale, believ'd of yore,
Chiefly rememb'ring the * ſweet ſong (whoſe ſtrain
Shall never die) of Him who wept in vain
" For his lov'd Lycidas," in the wide ſea
Whelm'd, when he cried, great Angel, unto thee,

* Alluding to Milton's Lycidas:—
        " But whether thou, to our moiſt vows denied,
        " Sleepſt by the fable of Bellerus old,
        " Or where the *viſion* of the *guarded Mcunt*
        " Looks to Namanco's and Bayona's hold,
        " Look homeward, Angel, now, and melt with ruth.

                Lycidas—*See Warton's excellent Note on the paſſage-*
                                Warton's Milton.

                                                    The

The fabled fcene of thy renown we trace,
And hail with thronging thoughts thy hallow'd refting-
 place!

THE ftealing Morn goes out—here let us end
Fitlieft our fong, and to the fhore defcend.

* YET once more, azure Ocean, and once more,
Ye lighted Headlands, and thou ftretching fhore,
Down on the beauties of your fcenes, we caft
A tender look, the longeft and the laft!

AMID the arch of Heav'n, extended clear,
Scarce the thin frecks of feathery clouds appear!
Beyond the long curve of the leffening bay
The ftill Atlantic ftretches its bright way,—
The tall fhip moves not on the tranquil brine!
Around, the folemn promontories fhine!

---

* " Yet once more, O ye laurels, and once more,
 " Ye myrtles brown," &c. LYCIDAS.

D

No

No founds approach us, fave, at times, the cry
Of the grey gull, that fcarce is heard fo high!
The billows make no noife, and on the breaft
Of charmed Ocean, Silence finks to reft!*

O might we thus from Heav'n's bright battlements
Behold the fcene Humanity prefents;
And fee, like this, all harmonis'd and ftill,
And hear no far-off founds of earthly ill;
Wide landfcape of the world, in pureft light
Array'd—how fair, how chearing were the fight!

---

* " A narrow ftone ftair cafe in one of the angles leads to the top of the
tower. The profpect hence is of fo grand a kind as to defy defcription,
and is perhaps as ftriking as any that can occur to " mortal eye," at the
fame height. The immenfe extent of fea which it exhibits raifes the moft
fublime emotions; the waves of the Britifh, Irifh, and Atlantic feas all roll
within the compafs of the fight, and the union of the two latter is inter-
rupted only by the bold eminences about the Land's-end. More under
the feet Penzance is diftinctly feen—the fcaffolding of the famous Wherry-
mine—and the hills eaftward of the bay uniting into a long rocky ridge."

Maton's Obfervations on the Weftern Counties.

ALAS!

ALAS! we think upon this feat of care,
And afk if peace, if harmony be there.
We hear the clangors and the cries, that fhake
The mad world, and their difmal mufic make!
We fee gaunt Vice, of dread enormous fize,
That fearlefs in the broad day fweltering lies,
And fcorns the feeble arrow that affails
His Heav'n-defying creft, and iron fcales!—
His brows with wan and wither'd rofes crown'd,
And reeling to the pipe's lafcivious found,
We fee Intemperance his goblet quaff;
And mocking Blafphemy, with mad loud laugh,
Acting before high Heav'n a direr part,
Sport with the weapons that fhall pierce his heart!

IF o'er the * fouthern wave we turn our fight,
More difmal fhapes of hideous woe affright!

* Alluding to the cruelties committed in France. Every Englifh heart
muft rejoice at the open, manly manner in which Mr. Sheridan avowed his
fentiments upon this fubject in the Houfe of Commons, April 20, 1798.

Grim-

* Grim-vifag'd War, that ruthlefs as he hies,
Drowns with his trumpet's blaft a brother's cries,
And Maffacre, by yelling furies led,
With ghaftly grin, and eye-balls rolling red!
O'er a vaft field wide heap'd with feftering flain,
Hark how the Dæmon Paffions fhout amain,
And cry, exulting, while the death-ftorm low'rs,
" Hurrah, the kingdoms of the world are ours!"

O God, who madeft man, I fee thefe things,
And wearied, wifh for a fleet Angels wings,
That I might fly away—and hear no more,
The furge that moans along this mortal fhore!"
But Joy's unclouded funfhine may not be,
Till, Father of all Worlds, we reft with Thee!
Then Truth, uplifting from thy works the pall,
Shall fpeak, " in wifdom haft thou made them all;"

* " Grim-vifag'd war."

Shakespeare.

Then

Then Angels, and Arch-angels, as they gaze,
And all th' acclaiming hoſt of Heav'n, ſhall raiſe
The loud Hoſannah of eternal praiſe!

HERE all is mixt with ſorrow—and the clouds
Hang awfully, whoſe ſhade the dim earth ſhrouds—
Therefore I mourn for man, and ſighing, ſay,
As down the ſteep I wind my home-ward way,
" O, when will Earth's long-muttering tempeſts ceaſe,
" And all be ſunſhine, like this ſcene, and Peace."

FINIS

ERRATA.

Page 6.—For *live*, read *lives* there, &c.

Page 9.—For " When heedlefs of the ftorm, &c."

Read " *While* heedlefs of the ftorm, &c."

Page 13.—For " Behold the painted warriors, &c."

Read " Behold the *dark-hair'd* warriors, &c."

Page 14.—For " And now far off, upon his watch of night,

" The mariner, &c."

Read " And now the failor, on his watch of night,

" Sees, like a glimm'ring ftar, the far-off light."

Page 15.—For " But truce to fancies—lo! our travels end,"

Read " *Of this no more*—lo! *here* our *journey ends*."

Page 17.—For " Melody pours forth her ten thoufand airs,"

Read " Melody pours forth her *winding* airs." *

Page 18.—*Note to* " Sick of the muling fentiment that fighs

" O'er its dead bird,† &c."

* Add as a *Note*—" Like the fongs of morning birds."

† Alluding to fuch pathetic hiftories as that of a dead canary bird, in a recent publication.

Quis taliâ fando,

Temperet a lacrimis?

———

In the Courſe of the Year will be publiſhed,

INSCRIPTIONS,

LATIN AND ENGLISH,

ACCOMPANIED WITH VIEWS TAKEN AT THE DIFFERERENT SCENES,

By the ſame Author,

AND ENGRAVED BY ALKIN.

—◆—

ALSO,

A SECOND VOLUME OF POEMS,

Printed uniformly with the Firſt Volume, Sixth Edition,

AS PUBLISHED BY CADELL AND DAVIES, STRAND.

———

S O N G

OF THE

BATTLE of the NILE.

PUBLISHED FOR THE BENEFIT OF

THE WIDOWS AND CHILDREN OF THE BRAVE

MEN WHO FELL

On that Memorable Day,

AND HUMBLY INSCRIBED

To the GENTLEMEN of the COMMITTEE.

———————————

BY THE

REV. W. L. BOWLES, A. M.

OF DONHEAD, WILTSHIRE,

AND RECTOR OF DUMBLETON, GLOUCESTERSHIRE.

———————————

L O N D O N:

PRINTED FOR T. CADELL, JUN. AND W. DAVIES, IN THE STRAND.

AND C. DILLY, IN THE POULTRY.

1799.

I.

SHOUT, for the LORD hath triumph'd gloriously!
  Upon the shores of that renowned land
  Where erst his " mighty arm, and out-stretch'd hand "
      He lifted high,
  And dash'd—" in pieces dash'd the enemy ;"—
      Upon that ancient coast
      Where " Pharaoh's chariots and his host "
      He cast into the deep,
  Whilst o'er their silent pomp he bid the swoln sea sweep ;
      Upon that Eastern shore
  That saw his awful arm reveal'd of yore,
AGAIN HATH HE ARISEN, and oppos'd
His FOES' defying vaunt.——O'er them the deep hath clos'd!

II.

  Shades of mighty chiefs of yore,
    Who triumph'd on the self-fame shore ;
  Ammon, who first o'er ocean's empire wide
  Didst bid the bold bark stem the roaring tide ;

² Sefac, who from the eaft to fartheft weft
Didft rear thy pillars over realms fubdu'd;
And thou ³, whofe bones do reft
In the huge pyramid's dim folitude,
Beneath the uncouth ftone,
Thy name and deeds unknown;
And Philip's glorious fon ⁴
With conqueft flufh'd, for fields and cities won;
And thou, Imperial Cæfar, whofe fole fway
The long-difputed world at laft confefs'd,
When on thefe fhores thy bleeding ⁵ rival lay;
O could ye, ftarting from your long cold reft,
Burft Death's oblivious trance,
And once again with plumed pride advance,
How would ye own your fame furpafs'd,
And on the fand your trophies caft,
When, the ftorm of conflict o'er,
And ceas'd the burning battle's roar,
Beneath the morning's orient light,
Ye faw, with fails all fwelling white,
Britain's proud fleet, to many a joyful cry,
Ride o'er the rolling furge in awful fovereignty!

III.

For fierce Ambition fir'd your mind——
 Befide your glittering car
 Amid the thickeft war,
Went Superftition, forcerefs blind,
In dimly-figur'd robe, with fcowling mien,
 ¹ Half-hid in jealous hood ;
And Tyranny, beneath whofe helm was feen
 His eye fuffus'd with blood ;
 And giant Pride,
That the great fun with haughty fmile defied ;
And Avarice, that grafp'd his guilty gold ;
 Thefe, as the forcerefs her loud fiftrum rung,
 Their difmal pæan fung ;
 And ftill, far off, pale Pity hung her head,
 Whilft o'er the dying and the dead
The victor's brazen wheels, with gory axle, roll'd.
 Now look on HIM,—in holy courage bold,—
 The affertor of his country's caufe behold !
 He lifts his gaze to heav'n, ferenely brave,
 And whilft around War's fearful banners wave,
He prays, " Protect us, as our caufe is juft,
" For in Thy might alone, Judge of the world ! we truft."

IV.

And they are fcatter'd—the deftroyers die!

THEY that ufurp'd the bloody victor's claim,

That fpoke of freedom, but " behold a cry!"

They, that like a wafteful flame,

Or the huge fandy pillar, that amain

Whirls 'mid the filence of the defert plain,

Deathful in their career of terror came!

And fcatter'd ruin as they pafs'd!

So rufh they, like the fimoom's horrid blaft.—

They fweep, and all around is wildernefs!

But from Thy throne on high,

Thou, GOD, haft heard the cry

Of nations in diftrefs!

Britain goes forth, beneath Thy might

To quell the proud blafphemers in the fight—

And Ægypt far along her winding main

Echoes the fhout of joy, and genuine Freedom's ftrain!

V.

Now let them, who Thy name, O God! defy,
    Invoke the mighty Prophet of the Eaſt,
    Or deck, as erſt, the myſtic feaſt
To Aſhtaoroth, queen of the ſtarry ſky!
        Let them, in ſome cavern dark,
        Seek Oſiris' buried ark;
Or call on Typhon¹, of gigantic form,
Lifting his hundred arms, and howling to the ſtorm;
        Or to that griſly king
        In vain their cymbals let them ring,
        To him in Tophet's vale rever'd,
        (With ſmoke his brazen idol ſmear'd,)
Grim Moloch, in whoſe fuming furnace blue
Th' unpitying prieſt the ſhrieking infant threw,
Whilſt to ſhrill cries, and drum's and timbrel's ſound,
The frantic and unhearing troop danc'd round;
        To *him*, deſpairing let them go,
And tell their fearful tale of hideous overthrow!

VI.

Calm breath'd the airs along the evening bay
      Where, all in warlike pride,
The Gallic fquadron ftretch'd its long array;
      And o'er the tranquil tide
   With beauteous bend the ftreamers wav'd on high:
But, ah! how chang'd the fcene e'er night defcends!
Hark to the fhout that heaven's high concave rends!
      Hark to the dying cry
   Of thoufands!—to the cannon's hollow roar,
   Heard far along the Nile's affrighted fhore;
      Where from his oofy bed
The cow'ring crocodile ' hath rais'd his head!
      What burfting flame
   Lightens the long tract of the gleamy brine?
      From yon proud fhip it came—
That tow'r'd the leader of the hoftile line!
Now loud explofion rends the midnight air!
Heard ye the laft deep groaning of defpair?—
Heaven's fiery cope unwonted thunders fill,
Then, with one dreadful paufe, earth, air, and feas are ftill!

VII.

But now the mingled fight
　　Begins its awful ſtrife again !
Thro' the dun ſhades of night
　　Along the darkly-heaving main
　　Is ſeen the frequent flaſh ;
And many a tow'ring maſt with dreadful craſh
Rings falling : Is the ſcene of ſlaughter o'er ?
　　Is the death-cry heard no more ?
Lo ! where the eaſt a glimmering freckle ſtreaks,
Slow o'er the ſhadowy wave the grey dawn breaks.
　　Behold, O ſun ! the flood
Strew'd with the dead, and dark with blood ! '
Behold, all ſcatter'd on the rocking tide,
The wrecks of haughty Gallia's pride !
　　But Britain's floating bulwarks with ſerene
　　And ſilent pomp, amidſt the deathful ſcene
　　Move glorious, and more beautiful diſplay
　　Their enſigns ſtreaming to thy orient ray.

B

VIII.

Awful Genius of the land,
 Who (thy reign of glory clos'd)
By marble wrecks, half-hid in fand,
 Haft mournfully repos'd ;
Who long, amidft the wafteful defert wide,
Haft lov'd with death-like ftillnefs to abide ;
 Or wrapt in tenfold gloom,
From noife of human things for ages hid,
 Haft fat upon the fhapelefs tomb
In the forlorn and dripping pyramid ;
 Awake ! Arife !——
Tho' thou behold the day no more
That faw thy pride and pomp of yore ;
Tho', like the founds that in the morning ray
 Trembled and died away,
From Memnon's ftatue ; tho' like thefe, the voice
That bid thy vernal plains rejoice,
 The voice of fcience is no longer heard ;
 And all thy gorgeous ftate hath difappear'd ;
Yet hear, with triumph, and with hope, again,
The fhouts of joy that fwell from thy forfaken main !

IX.

And, oh! might He, at whose command
Deep darkness shades a mourning land,
At whose command, bursting from night,
And flaming with redoubled light,
The Sun of Science mounts again
And re-illumes the wide-extended plain;
   Might He, from this eventful day,
      Illustrious Egypt! to thy shore
      Science, Freedom, Peace restore,
And bid thy crowded ports their ancient pomp display!
      No more should Superstition mark
      In characters, uncouth and dark,
   Her dreary, monumental shrine:
      No more should meek-ey'd Piety
      Outcast, insulted lie
Beneath the mosque whose golden crescents shine;
      But starting from her trance,
      O'er Nubia's sands advance
Beyond the farthest fountains of the Nile! [1]
The dismal Galla's should behold her smile,
And Abyssinia's inmost rocks rejoice
-To hear her awful lore, but soft consoling voice!

B 2

Davidson College Library

X.

Haſten, O GOD! the time, when never more
    Pale Pity, from her moonlight ſeat, ſhall hear
    (And dropping at the ſound a fruitleſs tear)
The far-off battle's melancholy roar;
When never more Horror's portentous cry
Shall ſound amid the troubled ſky;
Or dark Deſtruction's grimly-ſmiling mien,
Thro' the red flaſhes of the fight be ſeen!
Father in Heav'n! our ardent hopes fulfil—
Thou ſpeakeſt " Peace," and the vex'd world is ſtill!
       Yet ſhould Oppreſſion huge ariſe,
         And, with bloody banners ſpread,
         Upon the gaſping nations tread,
       Whilſt he Thy name defies,
    Truſting in Thee alone, we hope to quell
    His furious might, his purpoſe fell,
    And as the enſigns of his baffled pride
    O'er the ſeas are ſcatter'd wide,
We will take up a joyous ſtrain and cry
" SHOUT! FOR THE LORD HATH TRIUMPH'D GLORIOUSLY!"

FINIS.

N O T E S.

"Song of the Battle," &c.

I need not fay that Song, in this place, is ufed in its higheft fenfe, as a Lyrical compofition.

VERSE I.

¹ "Shout! for the Lord hath triumph'd glorioufly!"

EXODUS, Chap. xv.

Ver. 1. I will fing unto the Lord *for he hath triumphed glorioufly;* the *horfe and his rider* hath he thrown into the fea.——Ver. 4. Pharaoh's chariots and his hoft hath he caft into the fea.——Ver. 6. Thy right hand, O Lord, hath *dafhed in pieces* the enemy.—— Ver. 10. Thou didft blow with thy wind—the fea covered them : they fank as lead in the mighty waters.

VERSE II.

¹ "Ammon"

He was the firft that built long and tall fhips with fails—" Till then they ufed fmall and round veffels of burden on the Red Sea, and kept within fight of fhore." I follow the chronology of Sir Ifaac Newton.

² "Sefac"

1010 years before Chrift, Sefac, in the reign of his father Ammon, invades Arabia, and fets up pillars at the mouth of the Red Sea. 1008, invades Afric and Spain, and fets up pillars in all his conquefts, and particularly at the mouth of the Mediterranean. 971, invades India, and fets up pillars at the mouth of the Ganges.

³ "And thou, whofe bones do reft, &c."

The memory, fays Pliny, of thofe who built the pyramids, as a juft punifhment for their vanity, is buried in oblivion. It is well known, that in the loweft chambers of the largeft pyramid is a fepulchre cut out of entire ftone.

N O T E S.

⁴ " And Philip's glorious fon "

I fpeak of Alexander only as a conqueror: but I feel the truth of the learned Dr. Vincent's mafterly developement of his enlarged views, and fuperior character.

⁵ " Bleeding rival lay "

I need not, poffibly to any reader, mention the murder of Pompey, on the fhores of Ægypt, by which event the greateft part of the known world was poffeffed by Julius Cæfar. I cannot help adding, from Lucan,

　　" Cum Ptolemæorum manes, feriemque pudendam,
　" Pyramides claudant, indignaque maufolea :
　" Littora Pompeium feriunt, truncufqué vadofis
　" Huc illuc jactatur agnis."

Phar. Lib. viii.

Verse III.

¹ " Half-hid in jealous hood "

I mean by this expreffion merely to characterife, in general, the myftery and obfcurity of Ægyptian fuperftition, according to the idea of an ancient infcription in the temple of Ifis, at Sais :

　" I am whatever has been, is, and fhall be ; and no one *hath taken off my veil.*"

Verse IV.

¹ " Or the huge fandy pillar"

See Bruce's fublime defcription of the terrific appearance of the vaft columns of moving fand in the deferts.

² " Like the fimoom's horrid blaft "

See alfo Bruce's defcription of this peftilential wind.

Verse V.

¹ " Or call on Typhon, &c."

An Ægyptian deity. Apollonius fays he had an hundred heads ; and from his hundred mouths iffued devouring flames, and howlings fo dreadful that they terrified gods and men.

NOTES.

1 "Grim Moloch"

Syrian deity.—There was a burning furnace at the feet of his ftatue, into which they threw the children whom they offered to that god ; and whilft the miferable victim fhrieked as it burned to death, the priefts beat drums, &c. to hinder the cries from being heard. From this noife, the valley where it was moft frequently worfhipped was called " Tophet," the valley of difmal founds.

Abbé BANIER.

See Milton's fine defcription in his Hymn on the Nativity.

VERSE VI.

1 "The cow'ring crocodile hath rais'd, &c. "

I know that crocodiles are feldom feen below the falls, but I hope the idea may be excufed "poetice."

2 " Loud explofion rends the midnight air."

The burning of the L'Orient.

VERSE VII.

1 " Dark with blood "

μελαν αιμα. HOMER.

VERSE IX.

1 " Beyond the fartheft fountains of the Nile."

Πετρα υπο βλεμυων οθεν ουκετι Νειλος ορατος.

THEOCR. Idyl. 7. line 114.

Lately Published, by the same Author,

POEMS, in One Volume.   Sixth Edition.

ALSO

St. MICHAEL's MOUNT, a Poem written in Cornwall, 1797.

COOMBE ELLEN, a Poem, written in Radnorshire, Sep. 1798.

THE

SORROWS

OF

SWITZERLAND:

A POEM.

BY THE

REVEREND WM. LISLE BOWLES.

PRINTED FOR

T. CADELL, JUN. AND W. DAVIES, STRAND, AND J. MAWMAN, POULTRY, LONDON;

AND R. CRUTTWELL, BATH.

1801.

TO

MRS. WILLIAM DOUGLAS,

A NATIVE OF THE COUNTRY, WHOSE WRONGS THE FOLLOWING
LINES IMPERFECTLY DESCRIBE,

THIS POEM

IS RESPECTFULLY INSCRIBED

BY

HER SINCERE FRIEND AND SERVANT,

W. L. BOWLES.

DONHEAD,
MAY 25, 1801.

THE

SORROWS

OF

SWITZERLAND.

PART I.

WHY art thou come, Man of despair and blood,
       To these green vales, and streams o'erhung with wood?
These hills, where far from life's discordant throng,
The lonely goat-maid chaunts her matin song?
This cottag'd glen, where Age in peace reclines,
Sooth'd by the whisper of his native pines;
Where, in the twilight of his closing days,
Upon the glimmering lake he loves to gaze;
And like his life sees on the shadowy flood
The still sweet eve descending? Man of Blood!

Burst not his holy musings.   Innocence
And Peace these vales inhabit: hie thee hence
To the waste wilderness, the mournful main,
To caves, where silence and deep darkness reign,
(Where GOD's eye only can the gloom pervade)
And shroud thy visage in their dreariest shade!
Or if these scenes so beauteous may impart
A momentary softness to thine heart,
Let Nature plead—plead for a guiltless land—
Ere yet thou lift the desolating brand;
Ere yet thou bid the peaceful echoes swell
With havock's shouts, and many a mingled yell!
Pause yet a moment!   By the white white beard
Of him whose tear-red eyes to Heav'n are rear'd;
By her, who frantick lifts her helpless hand;
By those poor little-ones, that speechless stand—
If thou hast nature in thee, oh, relent!
Nor crush the lowly shed of virtue and content!

   No golden shrines can tempt thy plunder here;
No jealous castles their dark turrets rear.
Peeping at dawn among the mountain vines
The village-pastor's simple mansion shines,
Beneath the tower, the musick of whose bells
Soft o'er the azure lake each sabbath swells.
No taper'd halls, that blaze till morn, reply
To sounds of proud voluptuous revelry;

But one sweet pipe, by ling'ring lover play'd,
Cheers the dim valley, as the day-tints fade;
While in the rocks, the torrents, and the trees,
Her little world with pride Affection sees.

Survey the prospect well:—Soldier, dost THOU,
(Thy blood-red plumage rustling on thy brow)
Bid the poor villagers (who, in the shed
Of their forefathers, eat their virtuous bread)
To hard Oppression bend the prostrate knee,
Or learn BENEVOLENCE and LOVE from thee?

And dost thou talk of Freedom? Freedom here
Lifted, with death-denouncing frown, her spear—
Here, joining her loud voice's solemn call
To the deep thunders of the water-fall,
She hail'd her chosen home: these dark woods rung,
As her bold war-song on the rocks she sung—
At once a thousand banners to the air
Streaming, a thousand falchions brandish'd bare,
Proclaim'd her son's dread homage, "We will die,
" Or live thy children, holiest LIBERTY!"

Oh, think of this! Alas; the voice is vain!
Poor injur'd land! thy brave, thy blameless train;
Thy lovely landscapes; bursting bright around;
Thy glens, that echoed every cheering sound;
Thy rocks, that gleam'd with many a high-hung cot;
And FREEDOM's holy name, AVAIL THEE NOT!

Then rise, insulted Country—in despair
Lift thy brave arm more terrible—and swear,
Swear thou wilt never sheath th' avenging steel,
Till thou hast made the fell invader feel
How vain the terrors of his glitt'ring crest;
How warm the flame that fires a patriot's breast!
How nerv'd their arm, oppos'd to tenfold might,
Who for the dearest hopes, their homes, their offspring, fight!
And hark! e'en now, methought, stern Freedom call'd,
From the wild shores of rocky UNDERWALD!
    " Rush, like the mountain Avalanche,‡ on those
" Who, foes to you, my sons, are virtue's foes!
" Lo, where the legions of insulting FRANCE
" Already on your ravag'd plains advance;
" See your pale daughters—they for mercy plead;
" Behold your white-hair'd sires!—they sink—they bleed!
" Oh, yet your patriot energies unite,
" To quell the insolent oppressor's might!
" Behold the scene† where your forefathers broke,
" And sternly trampled on, the Austrian yoke!
" Behold the spot, where the undaunted band
" First met, and clasping each his brother's hand,
" Bade the ALMIGHTY hear their solemn vow:
' That never should their injur'd country bow

---

† The scene renowned by the names of Tell, Staffucher, &c.
‡ A mass of snow, that falls from the tops of the mountains.

' A slave!' then lifted in the midnight air
" Their spears, while the dun rocks reply'd, 'WE SWEAR.'
" Think that the DEAD behold you!—He† whose bow
" Laid the grim tyrant of these vallies low,
" On yonder eminence yet seems to stand,
" To YOU he dimly waves his awful hand.
" Go forth, my sons—in each bold bosom swell
" The injur'd spirit of another TELL;*
" And rush, like the huge Avalanche, on those
" Who, foes to you, are FREEDOM's, VIRTUE's foes."

So FREEDOM spoke; she stood august and high;
Like a pale meteor shone her troubled eye;
She smote her shield, and with indignant look
More awful her uplifted war-spear shook.

From many a wild and woodland solitude,
O'erhung with snowy-silver'd mountains rude;
From glassy lakes,· or where the bursting brook
Wells sparkling through some beech-embower'd nook;
From scatter'd shalots,† deck'd with mantling vines,
Above whose blue smoke wave th' impending pines;
From many a covert green, or gleamy rock,
The rude defenders of their country flock.

Upon a cliff, that at grey morning throws
Its shadow o'er the deep clear lake's repose,

---

* William Tell, founder of Swiss liberty.   † Peasants' Huts.

With firm yet sadden'd look, fix'd on the sun,
That now comes forth his glorious race to run,
Their holy leader* stands: " Children!" he cries,
(And one sad tear-drop gathers in his eyes)
" THEIR ARMS PREVAIL:—HELVETIA mourns in vain,
" Bound by the ruthless victor's griding chain;
" We only 'mid these rocky ramparts find
" Short shelter from the vultures of mankind:
" Hither they speed their desolating way,
" They flap their bloody'd pennons o'er their prey.
" But we have hearts, my brethren, and we know
" What to our country—to our GOD—we owe;
" And we have arms—arms that may make them rue
" (Though rude our ramparts, our defenders few)
" The hour when they assail'd this last retreat:
" Feel we our hearts leap high, our pulses beat?
" Death calls us—yet, oh lowly let us bend,
" And pray to Him, who is the poor man's friend,
" That He would guard our orphans when we bleed,
" And shield them in the bitter hour of need!"
   Now, soldier, let thy huge artillery roar,
Thy marshall'd columns flash along the shore;
Thy armed transports with long shadow ride
Terrifick o'er the lake's once-tranquil tide;

---

* Father Paul Stiger, leader of the Underwalders.

And thy loud trumpets bray, as in disdain
Of the poor tenants of the snowy plain!
　They fear thee not—they are Oppression's foes—
Unscar'd, thy march of carnage they oppose.
Though their fall'n brethren have in vain withstood,
Though yet thy sword be red with their best blood;
Thy sword, thy steeds, thy legions, they defy—
And death is couch'd within their flashing eye.
　Age has new energies—in traces weak
One angry hectick rises on his cheek;
And as his time-touch'd features kindling glow,
" Lead me," he cries, "yet lead me to the foe!"
Stern Manhood o'er his boy low-murm'ring bends,
Then, as his deadly weapon he extends,
Proudly exclaims, " Freedom or Death, my son!
" And thou, O God of Justice, lead us on!"
　Hark! with one shout they rush into the fight—
The pale foe shrinks before their gathering might!
Fragments of rocks in wild despair they wield,
And helms and shiver'd swords bestrew the field.
The frantick mother, hushing ev'ry grief,
Joins the dread scene, and to some plumed chief
(All pale with rage, with desperation wild)
Cries, as she smites his heart, " Hads't thou a child?"
　Unequal strife! the scene of death is o'er,
Mother and child lie side by side in gore!

When evening comes, through the lone cottage pane
No light looks cheerful in the dark'ning plain;
No pleasing sounds stray the dim hills along;
No home-returning goat-maid trills her song;
At intervals, wild accents of despair
Or shouts are heard, or dismal night-fires glare.
But all is dark and silent near the heap
Where the fallen heroes of the hamlet sleep;
Save that at times a hollow groan is heard,
Or melancholy cry of the night-bird;
Save where some dog, amidst the scene of death,
Moans, as he watches yet his master's breath;
While with despair, and love that seems to speak,
He licks the blood that stagnates on his cheek.
The moon looks through the hurrying clouds, the air
Sobs, as it lifts, at times, the dead man's hair;
Upon the mangled heaps the faint stars shine,
And Freedom sighs, "The triumph, GAUL, is thine!"
  How dawns the morn, o'er vales with blood defil'd,
Where late Affection's sweetest pictures smil'd!
O'er the still lake how sadly peals the bell,
That sounds of every earthly hope the knell!
  Pale o'er the bloody snows, without a home,
The sad survivors of the death-storm roam;
Their infants, outcast on the desert plain,
Demand their mothers and their sires in vain;

And when the red sun leaves the dark'ning sky,
Amid the gory tracts sit down and cry.

    Shores of LUCERNE! where many a winding bay
Shone beauteous to the morn's returning ray;
Where skyey tints upon the blue lake shone,
And touch'd the rocks with colours not their own;
Who now, with eyes that swim in tenderness,
The scenes, to ev'ry virtue dear, shall bless?
What pleasures now shall the rich landscape yield—
The sparkling cataract—the pendent field—
'Mid hoar declivities the sunny tow'r,
Peering o'er beeches that its roof embow'r;
And cottage-tops, with light smoke trailing slow
O'er the grey vapours looming far below?
Who shall ascend proud Pilate's* height, and mark
The motley clouds sail o'er the champagne dark,
Now breaking in fantastick forms, and now
Dappling the distant promontory's brow?
Then, when the sun that lights the scene, rides high,
And far away the scatter'd volumes fly,
Look up to the great GOD that rules the world,
By whom proud empires from their seats are hurl'd,
And feel a glow of holy gratitude,
That here, 'mid hollow glens, and mountains rude,

---

* Mount Pilate, on the Lake.

c

Far from Ambition's march, and Discord's yell,
Content, and Love, and Happiness, should dwell!
  Who now along those banks shall list'ning stray,
When evening lights each inlet west away,
And hear the solitary boatman's oar,
Dip duly, as he nears the shaded shore;
Or catch the whispers of the waterfall,
That through the ivy'd clefts swells musical.
These scenes, these sounds, could many a joy impart,
With sadness mix'd:—The wand'ring Youth, whose heart
Was sick with many sorrows, resting here
At such an hour, forgot his starting tear;
He felt a pensive calm, sweeter than sleep,
Steal gently o'er his aching breast; the deep,
And clear repose of th' unruffled lake
His spirit seem'd unconscious to partake;
And still the water, as it whisper'd near,
Or high-woods, as they rustled, sooth'd his ear,
Like the remembrance of a melody,
Heard in his infant happy days gone by.
Now in his distant country, when with tears
The tale of ruffian violence he hears—
Hears that the spot, which smil'd with lovely gleam,
Like some sweet image of a tender dream,
Upon his morning path, is drench'd with gore—
Its harmless tenants welt'ring on the shore!

He will exclaim, while from his breast he draws
A deep, deep sigh, "Avenge, O GOD! their cause."
  Who would not sigh for SWITZERLAND? What heart,
That ever bore in human woes a part;
That ever felt Affection's genuine flame;
That ever leap'd at injur'd Freedom's name;
Would not for her dark foes feel honest hate,
And swell with indignation at her fate?
  If thus her lot of sorrow have impress'd
Grief and resentment on a stranger's breast,
How must he hear the murd'rous tale of death,
He, who in these still vales first drew his breath!
'Tis his, perhaps, in distant climes to roam,
Far from the shelter of his early home;
Yet still, as fancy paints the spot, he sees
His father's cottage, and the mountain trees;
Again by the wild streams he seems to rove;
He hears the voice of her who won his love,
His heart's first love; for her he prunes the vine,
Whose clust'ring leaves the rustic porch entwine;
The mountains van together they ascend,
They see Alps pil'd on Alps, far on extend;
They mark the casual sunshine light the mass,
Or vernal show'rs along the valley pass;
Whilst, tinging the dark rocks, more lovely glow
The breeded colours of Heav'n's humid bow!

But now the maid he lov'd—with whom, all day,
He lov'd in summer o'er the hills to stray;
The faithful maid he lov'd—oh! cold despair
Freeze his warm life-blood; and that thrilling air*
Which erst he sung, when, all alive to joy,
He caroll'd on the Alps a peasant boy;
Let him not hear it now—lest his eyes start,
And madness harrow up his broken heart!

How touching was the simple strain: the tear
Of mem'ry started, when it met the ear;
And he whose front was rough with many a scar,
Whose bold heart bounded at the trump of war,
Stood all dissolv'd in sadness at its tone,
Rememb'ring him of pleasant seasons gone.

Perhaps full many a heavy hour had pass'd,
Since in its native nooks he heard it last;
And when again its well-known musick thrill'd,
A thousand thronging recollections fill'd
His soul, that, sick with longing, homeward rov'd:—
Remote from scenes which most on earth he lov'd,
Cast on a world tempestuous, bleak, and wide,
More ardent for his once-lov'd hills he sigh'd,
And sigh'd again, to think how it might fare
With sisters, brothers, friends, and parents there.†
But be its musick and its name forgot,
FOR DESERT IS HIS HOME, AND THOSE HE LOV'D ARE NOT.

---

* The famous *Rants de Vacches.*
† " And wakes to think how it might fare with you."   SHERIDAN.

PART II.

I Was a child of sorrow, when I pass'd,
Sweet Country, through your rocky vallies last;
For one whom I had lov'd, whom I had prest
With honest ardent passion to my breast,
Was to another vow'd: I heard the tale,
And to the earth sunk heartless, faint, and pale.
Till that sad hour when every hope was flown,
I thought she liv'd for me, and me alone.
Yet did I not, though pangs my heart must rend,
Prove to thy weakness a sustaining friend?
Did I not bid thee never, never more,
Or think of me or mine; as firm I swore
To cast away the dream, and bury deep,
As in oblivion of the dead man's sleep,
All that once sooth'd; and from the soul to tear
Each longing wish that youth had cherish'd there.

But when 'twas midnight, to the woods I hied
Despairing, and with frantic anguish cry'd:
" Oh! had relentless death with instant dart
" Smitten and snatch'd thee from my bleeding heart;
" Through life had niggard fortune bid us pine,
" And wither'd with despair my hopes and thine;
" Yes, yes, I could have borne it—but to see
" Th' accusing tear, and know it falls for me!
" O cease the thought—a long and last farewell—
" We must forget—nor shall my soul rebell!"
Then to my country's cliffs I bade adieu;
And what my sad heart felt, GOD only knew.
HELVETIA, thy rude scenes, a drooping guest
I sought; and, sorrowing, wish'd a spot of rest.
Through many a mountain-pass, and shaggy vale
I roam'd, an exile, passion-craz'd, and pale.
I saw your clouded heights sublime impend,
I heard your foaming cataracts descend;
And oft the rugged scene my heart endued
With a strange, sad, distemper'd fortitude;
Oft on the lake's green marge I lay reclin'd,
Murm'ring my moody fancies to the wind;
But when some hanging hamlet I survey'd,
Or wood-cot peeping in the shelter'd glade,
A tear perforce would steal; and, as my eye
Fondly reverted to the days gone by,

" How bless'd, (I cry'd) remote from every care
" To rest with her we lov'd, forgotten there!"
Then soft, methought, from the sequester'd grove
I heard the song of happiness and love:
   " Come to these scenes of peace,
    " Where to rivers murmuring
    " The sweet birds all the summer sing,
   " Where cares, and toil, and sadness cease!
   " Stranger, does thy heart deplore
   " Friends, whom thou wilt see no more?
   " Does thy wounded spirit prove
   " Pangs of hopeless sever'd love?
    " Thee the stream that gushes clear,
    " Thee the birds that carol near,
    " Shall soothe, as silent thou dost lye,
    " And dream to their wild lullaby.
   " Come to these scenes of peace,
   " Where cares and sadness cease."
  Start from the feeble dream! The woodland shed
Flames, and the tenants of that vale are dead!
All dark the torrent of their fate hath rush'd—
Each cheering echo of the plain is hush'd;
And every joyous, every tender sound
In the loud roaring of the night-storm drown'd!
  How cheerily the rocks from side to side
Oft to the tabor's festive sounds replied!

There, when the bells upon a holiday
Rung out, and all the villagers were gay,
In summer-time the happy groups were seen:
Youth link'd with beauty bounded on the green,
And Age sat smiling, as the joyous train,
(Round the tall May-tree* tap'ring from the plain)
Their locks entwin'd with ribbands streaming red,
And crown'd with flow'rs, the rural pastimes led;—
Oh! on the bleeding turf the poor flow'rs throw,
And weep for them that sleep in dust below.
There sleep together in their death-bed cold,
The beautiful, the brave, the young, the old!
No voice is heard that charm'd their earthly road:
Around their desolate and last abode,
The blast, that swept them to the earth, yet raves,
And strews with havock their insulted graves!

   As on the lucid lake's unruffled breast
Soft silv'ry lights, and blending shadows rest;
Above, around, the heaven's blue calm is spread,
And sleeps the sunshine on the mountain's head.
Then purple rocks and woods smile to the eye,
Like fairy landscapes of the ev'ning sky;
And all is still, save where some forest bird
With small and solitary trill is heard;

---

* May-Baum.

Sudden the scene is chang'd—the hurricane
Is up among the mountains—wind and rain
Drive, and strange darkness closes on the vale;
The high rocks to the light'ning glimmer pale;
And nought is heard, but the deep thunder's **roar,**
Or vultures screaming round the desert shore!
So mourns the prospect, chang'd and overcast,
And shrieks the spirit in the passing blast!

But ah! how feller bursts the ruthless storm,
That speeds the moral prospect to deform!
To-morrow, and the Man of Blood may see
Again fresh verdure deck the dripping tree;
Again pure splendour light the bursting views,
And the clear lake reflect the fairest hues;
Whilst the gay lark seems, with a livelier voice,
In scorn of his stern spirit, to rejoice.
But, hapless land! what day-spring shall restore
Thy lovelier morals that now smile no more.
Affection, tender as the murm'ring dove,
That in the noiseless wood her home-nest wove;
And Piety, that the blue mountains trod,
With kindling eyes uprais'd to nature's GOD!
Virtues that made thy streams, and woods, and hills,
Thy lakes, all sunshine, and thy shaded rills,
Like pictures of no earthly paradise!
Beaming remote from sorrow and from vice.

D

Child of the village pastor, modest sense,
And meekest piety, and innocence,
(If innocence in this hard world were seen)
Touch'd thy illumin'd eye, thy pensive mein,
As with a ray from heav'n.   Thy light loose hair
Hung gently-waving to the summer air;
Thy smiling cheek with health's rich glow was warm,
When with thy aged sire, arm link'd in arm,
Thou oft didst stray, beneath the beams of morn,
To gather herbs that the wild crofts adorn.
Meantime he taught thy inexperienc'd youth
Lessons of sober wisdom, and of truth;
He spoke of the great world beyond the vale—
Where uncouth shapes of want or woe assail;
He spoke of restless man's ungovern'd state—
And the dark-rushing torrent of his fate:
Then pointing to the craggy height, that shrouds
Its distant summit in the rolling clouds,
Bade thee revere th' ETERNAL ONE! (whose will
The earthquakes and the roaring deeps fulfill;
Whose awful thunder shakes th' astonish'd ball)
And trust in HIM, whatever fate befall!
   Oh! he did little think his shelter'd vale
Would prove the truest comment to the tale.
They tore her fainting from his aged side—
He miss'd the darling of his soul, and died!

For he sunk broken-hearted to the tomb—
Upon his grave no flowers in spring shall bloom;
Some with'ring weeds, perhaps, or scatter'd stones,
Mark the rude spot where they have cast his bones!
Soon, sad survivor, may thy sorrows cease,
And there thy heart be bury'd, and at peace,
Where thy poor father sleeps: till that blest day
When HE who saw your sufferings here, shall say,
" Come, children of affliction! love and joy
" Await you, where no griefs again annoy!
" Come, sainted children, and that bliss partake,
" Which HE alone can give who suffer'd for your sake."
    Far from the earthly scenes that wasteful lie,
Virtue, and Peace, and Arts, and Freedom fly.
Arts, which the wild surrounding views inspir'd;
And Freedom, such as genuine patriots fir'd.
When the great sun sinks in the crimson west,
And all the pines in golden pomp are drest;
Whose daring hand shall snatch the vivid light
That purples o'er the promontory's height;
And, with a LOUTHERBOURG's* rich pencil, throw
On the warm tablet all the lucid glow?
When the slow convent's bell sounds from afar,
And the dim lake reflects the ev'ning star;

* LOUTHERBOURG, a native of Switzerland.

List'ning to every farewell sound, that fills
The cottag'd glen beneath the pendent hills,
When shall again the rapt enthusiast rove,
And deck the visionary bower of love?

Hush'd be the Doric strain,† that, in the shade
Of his own pines, the pensive GESSNER play'd;
Which oft the homeward-plodding woodman near
Paus'd, with his grey beard on his staff, to hear;
Whilst his lean dog, whose op'ning lips disclose,
Just peeping forth, his white teeth's even rows,
Lifted his long ears with sagacious heed,
And fix'd his full eye on the trilling reed.
High on the broad Alps' solitary van,
Where not a sound is heard of busy man,
When shall again a silent HALLER lye,
And muse his theme coeval with the sky?

Hark! with loud orgies o'er the bloody dew,
Lewd Comus leads his nightly-madding crew!
Strange shouts and clangors through the high-wood run,
And distant arms flash to the sinking sun.

Dark forests their lone empire,* the tall rocks
Their shelter, and their wealth their wand'ring flocks,
To the proud Macedon, whose conquering car
Roll'd glorious through the armed ranks of war;

---

† GESSNER's Pastorals.

* I have taken this from PLANTA's interesting History of the Swiss Confederacy.

Whose banners chill'd the plain with fearful shade,
Whose sov'reignty a thousand trumpets bray'd,
The Scythian chiefs spoke nobly: "What have we,
" King of the world, to do with thine or thee?
" Far o'er the snowy solitudes we roam,
" Or by wild rivers fix our casual home;
" Nor heed the distant clarion of thy fame,
" Nor ask thy shouting legions whence they came.
" O'er the green champagne let thy cities shine,
" We ne'er invaded fields or seats of thine;
" Nor will we bow, proud Lord, at thy decree;
" Hence—hence—and leave us to our forests, free!"
    Oh, had such words, which simple freemen spoke,
Sav'd thee, HELVETIA, from the ruthless stroke
Of the stern soldier, who, with banners spread,
Through thy still vales his glitt'ring squadrons led!
But Heaven deny'd:—despair and murd'rous hate
Stalk o'er thy inmost vallies desolate!
And she, that like the nimble mountain-roe,
With step scarce heard, went bounding o'er the snow—
She, whose green buskins swept the frosts of morn,
Who wak'd the high wood with her bugle horn;
She, who once call'd these hills her own, and found
Her loveliest sojourn 'mid the hallow'd ground,
Blessing the spot, where shaded high with wood,
And deck'd with simple flowers, her altar stood;

FREEDOM insulted sees, as pale she flies,
A monster-phantom in her name arise!
On weltering carcases it seems to stand,*
Waving a dim-seen dagger in its hand;
Its look is unrelenting as the grave—
Around its brow the muttering whirlwinds rave—
Its stretching shadow chills the scene beneath—
Ah! fly—it onward moves, and murmurs "Death!"
Earth fades beneath its footstep, and around
Long sighs, and distant dying shrieks, resound!

Could arms alone o'er thy brave sons prevail,
HELVETIA? No—it was the fraudful tale
Of this false phantom, which the heart misled;
That spoke of peace—peace to the poor man's shed.
Then left him houseless to the tempest's gloom,
That swept his hopes and comforts to the tomb!
High tower'd the grisly spectre, half conceal'd,
And gath'ring clouds its dismal forehead veil'd.
The clouds disperse, and lo! 'mid murd'rous bands,
Dark in its might, the hideous phantom stands.
Now see the triumph of its reign complete,
Behold it throned in its sov'reign seat;
The orgies peal, the banners wave on high,
The dark rocks ring to shouts of liberty!

---

* Contrast between genuine Liberty and the spirit of Jacobinism.

Now, soldier, lift thy loud acclaiming voice!
Children of high-soul'd sentiment rejoice!
Round the scath'd tree upon the desert plain,
Dance o'er the victims of the village slain!
   Thou, who dost smiling sit, as Fancy flings
Her hues unreal o'er created things,
And as the scenes in gay distemper shine,
Dost wond'ring cry, "How sweet a world is mine!"
Ah! see the shades receding, that disclose
The direst spectacle of living woes!
And ye, who, all enlighten'd, all sublime,
Pant in indignant thraldom, till the time
When Man, bursting his fetters, proud and free,
The wildest savage of the wilds shall be;
Artful instructors of our feeble kind,
Illumin'd leaders of the lost and blind,
Behold the destin'd glories of your reign,
Behold yon flaming sheds—yon outcast train!
Hark! hollow-moaning on the fitful blast,
Methought, ROUSSEAU, thy troubled spirit past!
His ravag'd country his dim eyes survey,
"Are these the fruits" (he said, or seem'd to say)
"Of those high energies of raptur'd thought,
"That proud Philosophy my precepts taught!"
Then, shrouding his sad visage from the sight,
Flew o'er the cloudiest Alps to solitude and night.

Thou, too, who, musing history's vast plan,
Didst sit by the still waters of Lausanne,*
(What time Imperial Rome rose to thy view,
And thy bold hand her mighty image drew;)
Thou too, methinks, as the sad wrecks extend,
Dost seem in sorrow o'er the scene to bend.
With steady eye, and penetrating mind,
Thou hast survey'd the turmoil of mankind;
Hast mark'd Ambition's march, and fiery car,
And thousands groaning in the fields of war!
But direr woes might ne'er a sigh demand,
Than those of hapless injur'd Switzerland!
Oh! may they teach, whatever feelings start,
One awful truth,—that here we know in part!
Whatever darkness round his ark may rest,
There is a GOD, who knows WHAT IS IS BEST.
Submissive, still, adoring may we stand,
Beneath the terrors of his chast'ning hand;
And though dark clouds of carnage dim the sun,
Bend to the earth, and say, "Thy will be done."

---

* GIBBON finished his History on the banks of the Lake, in a summer-house.

THE END.

Cruttwell, Printer, Bath.

THE

PICTURE.

THE

P I C T U R E ;

VERSES WRITTEN IN LONDON,

MAY 28, 1803, SUGGESTED BY

A MAGNIFICENT LANDSCAPE OF

R U B E N S,

IN POSSESSION OF

SIR GEORGE BEAUMONT.

BY

THE REV. W. LISLE BOWLES.

LONDON:

PRINTED BY W. BULMER AND CO. CLEVELAND-ROW;
FOR MESSRS. CADELL AND DAVIES, STRAND; AND MR. JAMES
CARPENTER, BOND-STREET.
1803.

[*Price Two Shillings.*]

TO

LADY BEAUMONT

I HAVE a particular pleasure in inscribing these Verses; not so much on account of the kindness and hospitality I have myself experienced from her LADYSHIP *and* SIR GEORGE BEAUMONT, *as that I have an opportunity of making a small return of gratitude, for the greatest obligations, conferred by her Family, upon one who lives not to thank them—*MY FATHER.*

W. L. BOWLES.

May 29th, 1803.

---

* The Rev. William Thomas Bowles, presented to the livings of Uphill and Breane, Somerset, by John Willes, Esq.

THE PICTURE.

Nay, let us gaze, ev'n till the sense is full,
Upon the rich Creation, shadow'd so
That not great Nature, in her loftiest pomp
Of living beauty, ever, on the sight,
Rose more magnificent; nor aught so fair
Hath Fancy, in her wild and sweetest mood,
Imaged of things most lovely, when the sounds
Of this cold cloudy world at distance sink,
And all alone the warm idea lives
Of what is great, or beautiful, or good
In Nature's general plan!
        So vast the scope,
O Rubens, of thy mighty mind, and such
The fervor of thy pencil, pouring wide

The still illumination, that the mind
Pauses, absorb'd, and scarcely thinks what powers
Of mortal art the sweet enchantment wrought.
She sees the painter, with no human touch,
Create, embellish, animate, at will,
The mimic scenes, from Nature's ampler range,
Caught, as by inspiration, while the clouds,
High-wand'ring, and the fairest form of things
Seem, at his bidding, to emerge, and burn
With radiance and with life!

             Let us, subdued
Now to THE MAGIC OF THE MOMENT, lose
The thoughts of life, and mingle every sense
Ev'n in the scenes before us!

               The fresh morn
Of summer shines; the white clouds of the east
Are crisp'd; beneath, the bluey champaign steams;
The banks, the meadows, and the flow'rs, send up
An incens'd exhalation, like the meek
And holy praise of Him, whose soul's deep joy
The lone woods witness: Thou, whose heart is sick
Of vanities; who, in the throng of men,
Dost feel no lenient fellowship; whose eye
Turns, with a languid carelessness, around

Upon the toiling crowd, still murm'ring on,
Restless;—O think, in summer scenes, like these,
How sweet the sense of quiet gladliness,
That, like the silent breath of morning, steals
From lowly nooks, and feels itself expand
Amid the works of Nature, to the power
THAT MADE THEM: to the awful thought of HIM
Who, when the morning stars shouted for joy,
Bid the GREAT SUN from tenfold darkness burst,
The green earth roll in light, and solitude
First hear the voice of man, whilst hills and woods
Stood eminent, in orient hues array'd,
His dwelling,——and all living Nature smiled,
As in this pictured semblance, beaming full
Before us!

    Mark again the various view—
Some city's far-off spires and domes appear,
Breaking the long horizon, where the morn
Sits blue and soft: what glowing imagery
Is spread beneath!—Towns, villages, pale smoke,
And scarce-seen wind-mill sails, and devious woods,
Check'ring and chearing the grass-level land,
That stretches from the sight:
      Now nearer trace

The form of trees distinct, the broad brown oak,
The poplars, that, with paly trunks, incline,
Shading the lonely castle: flakes of light
Are flung behind the massy groups, that, now
Enlarging and enlarging still, unfold
Their separate beauties.—But awhile delay—
Pass the foot-bridge, and listen, (for we hear,
Or think we hear her,) listen to the song
Of yonder milk-maid, as she brims her pail,
Whilst in the yellow pasture, pensive near,
The red cows ruminate.—

Leave the loud, tumultuous throng,
And listen, listen, listen
To the milk-maid's simple song.

SONG.

" Forget me not, tho' forced to go
" Wide o'er the roaring sea ;
" When the night-winds blow,
" And the moon is high
" In the paly sky,
" My love, I will think of thee."

He look'd in my eyes, for I could not speak :
A tear he wiped from his dark-brown cheek.
  O then, my own true sailor said,
     " Though the roaring sea,
     " Part my love and me,
     " Yet if luck betide,
     " My bonny, bonny bride,
    " She shall be the young milk-maid."
O green are the rushes that flow'r in the burne,
And I grieve for my love, who may never return.

" Break off, break off,"* for lo ! where, all alarm'd,
The small birds,† from the late-resounding perch,
Fly various, hush'd their early song ; and mark,
Beneath the darkness of the bramble-bank
That over-hangs the half-seen brook, where nod
The flow'ring rushes, dew-besprent ; with breast,
Ruddy, and emerald wing, the king-fisher
Steals through the dripping sedge away : what shape
Of terror, scares the woodland habitants,
Marring the music of the dawn ? Look round,

---

  * Comus.
  † The Picture is on so large a scale, that all these circumstances are most
accurately delineated. The birds are chafinches, sparrows, &c.

See, where he creeps, beneath the willowy stump,
Cow'ring, and low, step silent after step,
The booted Fowler: keen his look, and fixt
Upon the adverse bank, while, with firm hand,
He grasps the deadly tube: his dog, with ears
Hung back, and still and steady eye of fire
Points to the prey; the boor, intent, moves on
Silent and creeping close, beneath the leaves,
And fears, lest ev'n the rust'ling reeds betray
His foot-fall: nearer yet, and yet more near
He stalks: Ah! who shall save the heedless groupe,
The speckled partridges, that in the sun,
On yonder hilloc green, across the stream,
Bask unalarm'd, beneath the hawthorn bush,
Whose aged boughs the crawling black-berry
Intwines!
    Alas, thus on the sweetest scenes
Of human loveliness, and social peace
Domestic, when the full fond heart reclines
Upon its hopes, and almost mingles tears
Of joy, to think that in this hollow world
Such bliss should be its portion; Then, (O hide
The fearful sight,) then, with his unheard step,
In darkness shrouded, yet approaching fast,

DEATH, from amidst the sunny flow'rs, lifts up
His giant dread Anatomy, and smites,
Smites the fair prospect once, whilst ev'ry bloom
Hangs rivel'd, and a sound of mourning fills
The lone and blasted valley : But no sound
Is here, of sorrow or of death, though she,
The country Kate, with shining morning cheek,
(Who, in the tumbril, with her market-geer,
Sits seated high,) seems to expect the flash
Exploding, that shall lay the innocent
And feather'd tenants of the landscape low.
Not so the clown, who heedless whether life
Or death betide, across the splashy ford
Drives slow ; the beasts plod on, foot following foot,
Aged and grave, with half-erected ears,
As now his whip above their matted manes
Hangs tremulous, while the dark and shallow stream
Flashes beneath their fet-locks : he astride
On harness-saddle, not a sidelong look
Deigns at the breathing landscape, or the maid
Smiling behind ; the cold and lifeless calf
Her sole companion ; and so mated oft
Is some sweet maid, whose thrilling heart was form'd
For dearer fellowship. But lift the eye,

And hail the abode of rural ease.—The man
Walks forth, from yonder antique hall, that looks
The mistress of the scene ; its turrets gleam
Amid the trees, and cheerful smoke is seen,
As if no spectred shape, (though most retired
The spot,) there ever wander'd, stol'd in white,
Along the midnight chambers ; but quaint Mab
Her tiny revels led, 'till the rare dawn
Peep'd out, and chanticleer his shrill alarm
Beneath the window rung, then, with a wink,
The shadowy rout are vanish'd !

                              As the morn
Jocund ascends, how lovely is the view
To him who owns the fair domain ! the friend
Of his still hours, is near, to whom he vow'd
His truth ; her eyes reflect his bliss : his heart
Beats high with joy : his little children play,
Pleased, in his path-way : one the scatter'd flow'rs
Straggling collects, the other spreads its arms,
In speechless blandishment, upon the neck
Of its caressing nurse :

                    Still let us gaze,
And image ev'ry form of heart-felt joy
Which scenes like these bestow, that charm the sight,

Yet sooth the spirit: all is quiet here,

Yet cheerful as the green sea, when it shines,

In some still bay, shines in its loneliness,

Beneath the breeze, that moves, and hardly moves

The placid surface.

On the balustrade

Of the old bridge, that o'er the moat is thrown,

The fisher, with his angle, leans intent,

And turns, from the bright pomp of spreading plains,

To watch the nimble fry, that glancing oft

Beneath the grey arch shoot! O happiest He

Who steals through life, untroubled as unseen!

The distant city, with its crouded spires,

That dimly shines upon his view, awakes

No thought, but that of pleasure more composed,

As the winds whisper him to sounder sleep.

He leans upon the faithful arm of Her

For whom his youthful heart beat, fondly beat,

When life was new: time steals away, yet health

And exercise are his; and in these shades,

Though sometimes he has mourn'd a proud World's wrong,

He feels an INDEPENDENCE that all cares

Breasts with a carol of content: he hears

The green leaves of his old paternal trees

Make music, soothing, as they stir: the elm,
And poplar with its silvery trunk, that shades
The green-sward of the bank, before his porch,
Are to him as companions,—while he turns,
With more endearment, to the living smile
Of those his infants, who, when he is dead,
Shall hear the music of the self-same trees
Waving, till years roll on, and their gray hairs
Go to the dust in peace.

           Turn from the thoughts—
See where the morning light, thro' the dark wood,
Upon the window-pane is flung, like fire.
HAIL, LIFE, and HOPE; but, THOU, great work of art,
That mid this populous and busy swarm
Of men, dost smile serene, as with the hues
Of sweetest, grandest Nature; mayst thou speak
Not vainly, of th' endearments and best joys
That Nature yields. The manliest heart that swells
With honest English feelings, (while the eye,
Sadden'd, but not cast down, beholds far off
The darkness of the onward-rolling storm,)
Charm'd for a moment by this mantling view,
Its anxious tumults shall suspend: and " SUCH,"
The pensive Patriot shall exclaim, " Thy scenes,

" My own beloved country, SUCH the abode

" Of rural peace! and while the soul has warmth,

" And voice has energy, the brave arm, strength,

" ENGLAND, THOU SHALT NOT FALL! The day shall come,

" Yes, and now is, that THOU shalt LIFT THYSELF,

" And woe to Him who sets upon thy shores

" His hostile foot! Proud Victor though he be,

" His bloody march shall never soil a flow'r

" That hangs its sweet head in the morning dew

" On thy green village banks! his muster'd hosts

" Shall be roll'd back in thousands, and the surge

" Bury them! Then, when PEACE illumes once more

" My country, thy green nooks and inmost vales,

" It will be sweet, amidst the forest-glens,

" To stray, and think upon the distant storm,

" That howl'd, but injured not!"

      Nor thoughts like these

Shall One, who bears an English heart, disown;

THOU shalt approve them, but thy nicer eye,

BEAUMONT, shall trace the master-strokes of art,

And view th' assemblage of the finish'd piece,

As with his skill, who form'd it: Darker views

Savage, with solitary pines, hung high

Amid the broken craggs, (where scowling wait

The fierce banditti,) stern Salvator's hand
Shall aptly shade: O'er Poussin's clust'ring domes,
With ampler umbrage, the black woods shall hang,
Beneath whose waving gloom the sudden flash
Of broken light, upon the brawling stream
Is flung below.

    Aërial Claude shall paint,
The gray fane peering o'er the summer woods,
The azure lake below, or distant seas,
And sails, in the pellucid atmosphere,
Soft-gleaming to the morn: Dark on the rock,
Where the red lightning bursts, shall WILSON stand,
Like mighty Shakspeare, whom the imps of fire
Await; nor oh, sweet Gainsborough, shall THEE
The Muse forget, whose simple landscape smiles
Attractive, whether we delight to view
The cottage chimney through the high wood peep,
Or beggar-beauty stretch her little hand
With look most innocent; or homeward kine
Wind thro' the hollow road at eventide,
Or brouze the straggling branches.

      Scenes like these
Shall charm all hearts, while truth and beauty live,
And Nature's pictured loveliness shall own

Each master's various touch; but chiefly THOU,
Great Rubens, shalt the willing senses lead,
Enamour'd of the varied imagery
That fills the vivid canvas, swelling still
On the enraptured eye of taste, and still
New charms unfolding; though minute, yet grand,
Simple yet most luxuriant, every light
And every shade, greatly opposed, and all
Subserving to one magical effect,
Of Truth and Harmony.

     So glows the scene;
And to the pensive thought refined, displays
The richest rural Poem: oh, may views
So pictured, animate thy classic mind,
Beaumont, to wander mid Sicilian scenes,
And catch the beauties of the Pastoral Bard,*
Shadowing his wildest landscapes.—Ætna's fires,
Bebrycian rocks, Anapus's holy stream,
And woods of ancient Pan: the broken crag
And the old fisher here; the purple vines
There bending; and the smiling boy,† set down

---

* Theocritus. Alluding to a design of illustrating the PICTURESQUE CHA-
RACTER of the venerable Sicilian, by paintings of Sir George, from new trans-
lations of Messrs. Sotheby, Rogers, Howley, W. Spencer, and the author.
† Landscapes taken from the First Idyll of Theocritus.

To guard, who, innocent and happy, weaves,

Intent his rushy basket, to ensnare

The chirping grass-hoppers, nor sees the while

The lean fox meditate her morning meal,

Eying his scrip askance, whilst farther on

Another treads the purple grapes—he sits,

Nor aught regards, but the green rush he weaves!

   O Beaumont, let this pomp of light and shade

Wake thee, to paint the woods, that the sweet Muse

Has consecrated : then the summer-scenes

Of Phasidamus,* clad in richer light,

Shall glow, the glancing poplars, and clear fount;

While distant times admire (as now we trace

This lovely-spreading view) dark Ætna's pines,

The nymph's cool grotts, and branching planes, that shade

The silver Arethusa's stealing wave.

* See the exquisite Landscape in the Seventh Idyll.

THE END.

Printed by W. Bulmer and Co.
Cleveland-row, St. James's.

Bowden Hill;

THE BANKS OF THE WYE,

Cadland,

SOUTHAMPTON RIVER.

———————

By the Rev. W. LISLE BOWLES, *A. M.*

Rector of Dunbleton, Gloucestershire; Brembill, Wilts; Prebendary of Sarum;
and Chaplain to His Royal Highness the Prince of Wales.

———————

Baker and Fletcher, Printers, Southampton.
June 1806

𝕭𝖔𝖜𝖉𝖊𝖓 𝕳𝖎𝖑𝖑.

Inscribed to the MARCHIONESS *of* LANSDOWNE.

HOW cheering are thy profpects, airy Hill,
To him who, cold and languid on thy brow,
Paufes, refpiring! winding through the fhade
Of woods, that fweep with mazy track the verge
Of LANSDOWNE's proud domain,* upon the point
Of the defcending fteep I ftand!

                              So Rich,
So mantling in the gay and gorgeous hues
Of Summer; far beneath me, fpreading wide
From Field to Field from Vale to cultur'd Vale;
Here, white with paffing Sunfhine; There, with trees
Innumerable fpeckled, till they blend,
Loft in the azure Diftance, lives the Scene!

    Lives! all is Life, all Beauty! from the Grave
Whofe fleep is dark and dreamlefs, fnatch'd fo late,
Shall I pafs filent, now firft iffuing forth,†
To tafte again thy Beauties, to refpire
Thy Breath; to hail thy look, thy living look,
O Nature? let me the deep Joy contraft,
(Which now the inmoft Breaft, like Mufic, fills,)
With the fick Chamber's Sorrows, oft from morn,
Silent, till lingering Eve, fave when the found
Of whifpers fteal, and bodings breath'd more low
As friends approach the Pillow; fo awak'd
From deadly Trance, the fick Man lifts his Eyes,
Then in Defpondence clofes them on all,

* Bowood.

† After two months' confinement, from illnefs.

All Earth's fond wifhes! O how chang'd are now,
His Thoughts! he fees rich Nature kindling round,
He feels her Influence! languid with delight,
(And whilft his Eye is fill'd with tranfient Fire,)
He almoft thinks he hears her gently fay,
Live, Live! Oh Nature, Thee in the foft winds,
Thee, in the foothing found of Summer leaves,
When the ftill Earth lies fultry; Thee, methinks,
Ev'n now I hear bid "Welcome" to thy Vales
And Woods again!
     And I will welcome them
And pour, as erft the Song of heart-felt Praife.

 From yonder line, where fade the fartheft Hills
Which bound the blue lap of the fwelling Vale,
On whofe laft line, feen folitary, hangs
Thy tow'r,* benevolent, accomplifh'd Hoare,
To where I ftand, how wide the Interval!
Yet inftantaneous, to the hurrying Eye
Difplay'd; though peeping Tow'rs and Villages
Thick fcatter'd, mid' the intermingling Elms,
And Towns remotely mark'd by hovering Smoke
And grafs-green Paftures with their Herds, and Seats
Of rural Beauty, Cottages and Farms,
Unnumber'd as the Hedgerows, lie between!
 Roaming at large to where the grey Sky bends,
The Eye fcarce knows to reft, till back recall'd
By yonder Ivied Cloifters† in the Plain,

* Sir Richard Hoare's tower.   † Lacock Abbey.

Whose Turret peeping pale above the Shade,
Smiles in the venerable Grace of Years.
As the few threads of Age's silver hairs,
Just sprinkled o'er the Forehead, lend a Grace
Of faintly Reverence, seemly, though compar'd
With young Belinda's clust'ring Tresses brown;
So the grey weather-stained Tow'rs yet wear
A secret Charm impressive; though oppos'd
To Views in verdure flourishing, the Woods,
And Scenes of attic Taste, that glitter near.*

 O! VENERABLE PILE,† though now no more
The pensive Passenger, at Evening, hears
The slowly chanted Vesper; or the Sounds
Of "MISERERE," die along the Vale;
Yet PIETY and HONOUR'D AGE retired,
There hold their blameless Sojourn, ere *the Bowl*
" *Be broken, or the silver Chord be loos'd.*"

 Nor can I pass, snatch'd from untimely Fate,
Without a secret Pray'r, that so my Age
May wait its close,—so honour'd so rever'd!

 May I yet breathe, alive to Nature's Charms,
And though no pealing Clarion swell my Fame
When Life's brief Tale is told; let me not pass,
Like the forgotten Clouds of Yesterday,
Nor unremember'd by the fatherless,
In the poor Village where my Bones are laid.§

* Bowood, and Mr. Dickenson's.

† Lacock Abbey.   § Bremhill.

June 10, 1806.

THE BANKS OF THE WYE.

To Miss Morrison.

THE funshine of summer the hills was adorning,
  And languor and sicknels and pain seem'd to fly,
As cheer'd by the beams and the incenfe of morning,
  I wander'd, fo pale, on the banks of the Wye:
O ftill, lovely Wye, when, with fighs unavailing,
We think of the health and the ftrength that is failing,
May'ft thou footh him who flow on thy bofom is failing,
  Forgetful of all, but the fcenes of the Wye.

Befide the vaft mountain, yet drooping in danger,
  I pour'd the cold waters of MALVERN in vain;
Was fad in the crowd, where each heart was a
    ftranger,
  And caft my eyes aching o'er all the proud plain:
Then oh, lovely Wye, to the fpirit how cheering,
Thy meads and thy woods how delightful appearing,
To him, who no longer the PHANTOM is fearing,
  Which vanifh'd, like night, on the waves of the Wye!

With hope and delight while the bofom is burning,
  But one tender wifh claims a fhare in my heart,
That THEY too may find health and pleafure returning,
  From whom I was forry (how forry!) to part:
With ardor and joy while the heart thus is fwelling,
The thoughts on the diftant with tendernefs dwelling,
Nor Fancy the gloom of the Future foretelling,
  How pleafant the fcenes on the banks of the Wye!

Monmouth, July 24, 1806.

Written at Cadland,

Southampton River.

To Andrew Drummond, Esq.

IF ever sea-maid, from her coral cave,
Beneath the hum of the great surge, has lov'd
To pass delighted from her green abode,
And seated on a summer bank, to sing
No earthly music: in a spot like this,
Fancy might think she heard her, as she dry'd
Her golden Hair, yet dripping from the main,
In the slant sun-beam:

                    So the pensive Bard
Might shadow, warm'd with this enchanting scene,
Th'Ideal Form; but, tho' SUCH THINGS ARE NOT,
HE, who has ever felt a thought refin'd;
HE, who has wander'd on the sea of Life,
Forming delightful visions of a Home,
Of beauty and repose;—He, who has lov'd,
With filial warmth his country, will not pass
Without a look of more than tenderness
On all the scene; from where the pensile Birch
Bends on the Bank, amid the cluster'd group
Of the dark Hollies; to the woody shore
That steals diminish'd, to the distant spires
Of Hampton, crowning the long lucid wave.
White in the sun, beneath the edging shade,
Full shines the frequent sail, like Vanity,
As she goes onward in her glittering trim,

Amid the glances of life's tranfient morn,
Calling on all to view her.

     Vectis there,*
That flopes its green-fward to the lambent wave,
And fhows thro' fofteft haze its woods and domes,
With grey St. Catharine's creeping to the fky,
Seems like a modeft Fair, who ch: *ns the more,
Concealing half her beauties.

     To the Eaft,
Proud, yet complacent, on its fubject realm,
With mafts innumerable throng'd, and hulls
Seen indiftinct, but formidable, mark,
Albion's vaft fleet, that, like the impatient ftorm,
Waits but the word, to thunder and flafh DEATH
On HIM, who dares approach, to violate
The fhores and living fcenes that fmile fecure
Beneath its Dragon-Watch!

    LONG MAY THEY SMILE!
And long, majeftic Albion, (while the found
From Eaft to Weft, from Albis† to the Po,
Of dark contention hurtles,) mayft thou reft,
As calm and beautiful this fylvan fcene,
Looks on the refluent wave that fteals below.

   * The Ifle of Wight. † The Elba.

Sept. 21, 1806.

Baker and Fletcher, Printers, Southampton.

THE

GRAVE OF THE LAST SAXON;

OR,

THE LEGEND OF THE CURFEW.

LONDON:

PRINTED BY THOMAS DAVISON, WHITEFRIARS.

THE

GRAVE OF THE LAST SAXON;

OR,

THE LEGEND OF THE CURFEW.

A POEM.

BY THE REV. W. L. BOWLES,

AUTHOR OF LETTERS TO LORD BYRON,
POEMS, ETC.

LONDON:

PRINTED FOR HURST, ROBINSON, AND CO.;

AND

ARCHIBALD CONSTABLE AND CO., EDINBURGH.

1822.

TO

RICHARD HEBER, ESQ.,

M. P. FOR THE UNIVERSITY OF OXFORD,

THIS POEM IS DEDICATED,

IN TOKEN OF PUBLIC AND PRIVATE RESPECT,

BY HIS OBEDIENT SERVANT,

W. L. BOWLES.

INTRODUCTION.

THE circumstance of the late critical controversy with Lord Byron having recalled my attention to a poem, sketched some years ago, on a subject of national history, I have been induced to revise and correct, and now venture to offer it to the public.

The subject, though taken from an early period of our history, is, as far as relates to the Grave of Harold, purely imaginary, as are all the characters, except those of the Conqueror, and of Edgar Atheling. History, I think, justifies me in representing William as acting constantly under strong religious impressions. A few circumstances in his life will clearly show this. When Harold was with him in Normandy, he took an oath of him on *two* altars, within which were concealed miraculous relics *. His banner was sent from Rome, consecrated by the Pope, for the especial purpose of the invasion of England. Without adverting to the night spent in prayer before the battle of Hastings, was not this impression more decidedly shown when he pitched his tent among the dead on that night, and vowed to build an abbey on the spot? The event of the battle was so much against all human probability, that his undertaking it, at the place and time, can only be reconciled by supposing he acted under some extraordinary impression.

When the battle was gained, he knew not on what course to determine: instead of marching to London, he retired towards Dover. When he was met by the Kentish men, with green boughs, the quaint historian says, " He was *daunted.*" These and many other incidental circumstances may occur to the reader.

* See the picture in Stodhard's travels.

In representing him, therefore, as under the control of superstitious impressions, I trust I have not transgressed, at least, poetical *verisimilitude*. An earthquake actually happened about the period at which the poem commences, followed by storms and inundations. Of these facts I have availed myself.

I fear the poem will be thought less interesting, from having nothing of *Love* in it, except, in accordance with the received ideas of the gentleness of Atheling's character, I have made him not insensible to one of my imaginary females, and have therefore, to mark his character, made him advert to the pastoral scenes of Scotland, where he had been a resident. There is a similarity between my "Monk," and "The Missionary," but their offices and the scenes are entirely different, and some degree of similarity was unavoidable in characters of the same description.

Filial affection, love of our country, bravery,

sternness, (inflexible, except under religious fears,) the loftier feelings of a desolate female, under want and affliction, with something of the wild prophetical cast; religious submission, and deep acquiescence in the will of God; these passions are brought into action, round one centre, if I may use the word, "The GRAVE OF THE LAST SAXON."

That Harold's sons landed with a large fleet from Denmark, were joined by an immense confederate army, in the third year of William's reign, is a well-known historical fact. That York was taken by the confederate army, and that all the Normans, except Sir William Malet, and his family, were killed, is also matter of record. (*See Drake's History of York, and Turner's History of England.*) That afterwards (the blow against William failing), the whole country, from the Humber to Tyne, from the east to the west, was depopulated by sword and famine, are facts also found in all historians.

Some slight anachronisms may, I hope, be pardoned; if anachronisms they are, such as the year in which the Tower was built, &c.

The plan will be found, I trust, simple and coherent, the characters sufficiently marked and contrasted, and the whole, conducive, however deficient, in other respects, to the excitement of virtuous sympathy, and subservient to that, which alone can give dignity to poetry, the cause of moral and religious truth.

ERRATA.

Page 35, line 16.

To

　　"Mingled with things forgotten,"

Add

　　　　　　　"Until the
　　"And then remember'd freshly."

Page 37, line 9.

For

　　　　　　　　"This,
　　"Your darling, for his safety, lo!"

Read

　　　　　　　　"Him,
　　"Whom ev'ry eye must view with tendernes
　　"Oh! trust me; for his safety, lo! I pledge."

Page 45, line last, *dele* "rose."
　　75,　　6, *dele* "midnight."
　　86,　　2, *for* "warm," *read* "warn."

The Grave of the last Saxon;

OR,

THE LEGEND OF THE CURFEW.

The Grave of the last Saxon.

INTRODUCTORY CANTO.

*Subject—Grave and Children of Harold—Confederate
Army of Danes, Scots, and English arrived in the
Humber the third year of the Conqueror, and marching
to York.*

" KNOW ye THE LAND where the bright orange glows?"

Oh! rather know ye not THE LAND, belov'd

Of Liberty, where your brave fathers bled?

THE LAND of the white cliffs, where ev'ry cot

Whose smoke goes up in the clear morning sky,

On the green hamlet's edge, stands as secure

As the proud Norman castle's banner'd keep?

Oh! shall the poet paint a land of slaves,

(Albeit, that the richest colours warm

His tablet, glowing from the master's hand,)

And THEE forget, HIS COUNTRY—thee, HIS HOME?

Fair Italy! thy hills and olive-groves,
A lovelier light empurples—or when Morn,
Streams o'er the cloudless van of Apennine,
Or more majestic Eve, on the wide scene,
Of columns, temples, arcs, and aqueducts,
Sits, like reposing Glory, and collects
Her richest radiance at that parting hour;
While distant domes, touch'd by her hand, shine o
More solemnly, 'mid the gray monuments,
That strew th'illustrious plain; yet say, can these,
E'en when their pomp is proudest, and the sun,
Sinks o'er the ruins of Immortal Rome,
A holy int'rest wake, intense as that,
Which visits his full heart, who, sever'd long,
And home returning, sees once more the light
Shine on the land where his forefathers sleep;
Sees its white cliffs at distance, and exclaims,
" There I was born, and there my bones shall rest?

Then, oh! ye bright pavilions of the East,
Ye blue Italian skies, and summer-seas,

By marble cliffs high-bounded, throwing far
A gray illumination through the haze.
Of orient morning; ye, Etruscan shades,
Where Pan's own pines o'er Valombrosa wave;
Scenes, where old Tiber, for the mighty dead
As mourning, heavily rolls; or Anio
Flings its white foam; or lucid Arno steals
On gently through the plains of Tuscany;
Be ye th' impassion'd themes of other song.

Nor mine, thou wond'rous WESTERN WORLD, to call
The thunder of thy cataracts, or paint
The mountains and the vast volcano-range
Of Cordilleras, high above the stir
Of human things, lifting to middle air
Their snows in everlasting solitude,
Upon whose nether crags the vulture, lord
Of summits inaccessible, looks down,
Unhearing, when the thunder dies below!

Nor, midst th' irriguous valleys of the South,
Where Chili spreads her green lap to the sea,

Now pause I to admire the bright blue bird,
Brightest and least of all its kind, that spins
Its twinkling flight, still humming o'er the flow'rs,
Like a gem of flitting light!

     TO THESE ADIEU!
Yet ere thy melodies, my harp, are mute
For ever, whilst the stealing day goes out
With slow-declining pace, I would essay
One patriot theme, one ancient British song:
So might I fondly dream, when the cold turf
Was heap'd above my head, and carping tongues
Were ceased, some tones, OLD ENGLAND, thy green hills
Might then remember———

———

    TIME HAS REFT THE SHRINE,
Where the LAST SAXON, canonized, lay,
And every trace has vanish'd, like the light
That from the high-arch'd eastern window fell,
With broken sunshine, on his marble tomb—

So have they pass'd; and silent are the choirs
That to his spirit sung eternal rest;
And scatter'd are his bones who raised those walls,
Where, from the field of blood slowly convey'd,
His mangled corse, with torch and orison,
Before the altar, and in holy earth,
Was laid! Yet oft I muse upon the theme,
And now, whilst solemn the slow curfew tolls,
Years and dim centuries seem to unfold
Their shroud, as at the summons; and I think
How sad that sound on ev'ry English heart
Smote, when along those dark'ning vales, where Lea [1]
Beneath the woods of Waltham winds, it broke
First on the silence of the night, far heard
Through the deep forest! PHANTOMS OF THE PAST,
Ye gather round me! VOICES OF THE DEAD,
Ye come by fits! And now I hear, far off,
Faint ELEESONS swell, while to the fane
The long procession, and the pomp of death,
Moves visible; and now one voice is heard

From a vast multitude, " Harold, farewell!

" Farewell, and rest in peace!"   That sable car

Bears the LAST SAXON to his grave, (the last

From Hengist, of the long illustrious line

That sway'd the English sceptre!)   Hark! a cry!

'Tis from his mother, who, with frantic mien,

Follows the bier! with manly look composed,

Godwin, his eldest-born, and Adela,

Her head declined, her hand upon her brow

Beneath the veil, supported by his arm,

Sorrowing succeed: lo! pensive Edmund there,

Leads Wolfe, the least and youngest, by the hand!—

Brothers and sisters, silent and in tears,

Follow their father to the dust, beneath

Whose eye they grew—Last and alone, behold,

Marcus, (2) subduing the deep sigh, with brow

Of sterner acquiescence—Slowly pace

The sad remains of England's chivalry,

The few whom Hastings' field of carnage spared,

To follow their slain monarch's hearse this night,

Whose corse is borne beneath th' escutcheon'd pall,

To rest in Waltham Abbey.   So the train,

(Imagination thus embodying it)

Moves onward to the Abbey's western porch,

Whose windows and retiring aisles reflect

The long funereal lights.   Twelve stoled monks,

Each with a torch, and pacing, two and two,

Along the pillar'd nave, with crucifix

Aloft, begin the supplicating chant,

Intoning " Miserere Domine."

Now, the stone-coffins in the earth are laid

Of Harold, and of Leofrine, and Girth, (3)

Brave brethren slain in one disastrous day.

And hark! again the monks and choristers

Sing, pacing round the grave-stone, " REQUIEM

" ETERNAM DONA IIS."—TO HIS GRAVE,

So was King Harold borne, within those walls

His bounty raised: his children knelt and wept,

Then slow departed, never in this world,

Perhaps, to meet again.   But who is she,
Her dark hair streaming on her brow, her eye
Wild, and her breast deep-heaving? She beheld
At distance the due rites, nor wept, nor spake,
And now is gone.

              Alas! from that sad hour,
By many fates, all who that hour had met,
Were scatter'd.   Godwin, Edmund, Adela,
Exiles in Denmark, there a refuge found
From England's stormy fortunes.   Three long years
Have pass'd; again they tread their native land.—
The Danish armament beneath the SPURN ⁽⁴⁾
Is anchor'd—Twenty thousand men at arms
Follow huge Waltheof, on his barbed steed,
His battle-axe hung at the saddle bow;—
Morcar and Edwin, English earls, are there,
With red-cross banner, and ten thousand men
From Ely and Northumberland: they raise
The death-song of defiance, and advance
With bows of steel.   From Scotland's mountain-glens,

From sky-blue lochs, and the wild highland heaths,

From Lothian villages, along the banks

Of Forth, King Malcolm leads his clansmen bold,

And, dauntless as romantic, bids unfurl

The banner of St. Andrew! by his side

Mild Edgar Atheling, a stripling boy,

His brother, heir to England's throne, appears,

The dawn of youth on his fresh cheek! and lo!

The broad-swords glitter as the tartan'd troops

March to the pibroch's sound.   The Danish trump

Brays, like a gong, heard to the holts and towns

Of Lincolnshire.

                With crests and shields the same,

A lion frowning on each helmet's cone,

Like the two brothers famed in ancient song, [5]

Godwin and Edmund, sons of Harold, lead

From Scandinavia and the Baltic isles

The impatient Northmen to th' embattled host

On Humber's side—The standards wave in air,

Drums roll, and glittering columns file, and arms

Flash to the morn, and banner'd-trumpets bray,

Heralds, or armorers, from tent to tent

Are hurrying—crests, and spears, and steel-bows gleam,

Far as the eye can reach—barb'd horses neigh—

Their mailed riders wield the battle-axe,

Or draw the steel-bows with a clang—and hark!

From the vast moving host is heard one shout,

" CONQUEST or DEATH !"—as now the sun ascends,

And on the bastion'd walls of Ravenspur

Flings its first beam—one mighty shout is heard,

" PERISH THE NORMAN! SOLDIERS, ON!—TO YORK!"

The Grave of the last Saxon.

CANTO THE FIRST.

Castle of Ravenspur, on the Humber — Daughter of Harold — Ailric, the monk.

" LET us go up to the west turret's top,"
Adela cried; " let us go up—the night
" Is still, and to the east great ocean's hum
" Is scarcely heard. If but a wand'ring step,
" Or distant shout, or dip of hast'ning oar,
" Or tramp of steed, or far-off trumpet, break
" The hush'd horizon, we can catch the sound,
" When breathless expectation watches there."

Upon the platform of the highest tow'r
Of Ravenspur, beneath the lonely lamp,

At midnight, leaning o'er the battlement,

The daughter of slain Harold, Adela,

And a gray monk who never left her side,

Watch'd: for this night or death or victory

The Saxon standard waits——

                  Hark! 'twas a shout,

And sounds at distance as of marching men!

No! all is silent, save the tide, that rakes,

At times, the beach, or breaks beneath the cliff.

Listen! was it the fall of hast'ning oars?

No! all is hush'd! "Oh! when will they return?"

Adela sigh'd; for three long nights had pass'd,

Since her brave brothers left these bastion'd walls,

And march'd, with the confederate host, to York.

"They come not: Have they perish'd?" So dark thoughts

Arose, and then she rais'd her look to Heav'n,

And clasp'd the cross, and pray'd more fervently.

Her lifted eye in the pale lamp-light shone,

Touch'd with a tear; soft airs of ocean blew

Her long light hair, whilst audibly she cried,

" Preserve them, blessed Mary! oh! preserve

" My brothers."   As she pray'd, one pale small star,

A still and lonely star, through the black night

Look'd out, like Hope!—Instant, a trumpet rung,

And voices rose, and hurrying lights appear'd;

Now louder shouts along the platform peal—

" Oh! they are Normans!" she exclaim'd, and grasp'd

The old man's hand, and said, " yet we will die

" As HAROLD'S DAUGHTER;" and, with mien and voice,

Firm and unfaltering, kiss'd the crucifix.

They knelt together, and the old man spoke:

" All here is toil and tempest—we shall go,

" Daughter of Harold, where the weary rest."

Oh! holy Mary, 'tis the clank of steel

Up the stone stairs! and, lo! beneath the lamp,

In arms, the beaver of his helmet raised,

Some light hairs straying on his ruddy cheek,

With breath hastily drawn, and cheering smile,

Young ATHELING.   " THE SAXON BANNER WAVES"—

" Oh! are my brothers safe?" cried Adela,

" Speak! speak! Oh! tell me, do my brothers live?"

Atheling answer'd, " They will soon appear—

" My post was on the eastern hills—a scout

" Came breathless, sent from Edmund, and I hied,

" With a small company, and horses fleet,

" At his command, to thee.   He bade me say,

" Even now, upon the citadel of York,

" Above the bursting fires, and rolling smoke,

" THE SAXON BANNER WAVES"——

                        " I thank thee, Lord!

" My brothers live!" cried Adela, and knelt

Upon the platform, with uplifted hands,

And look to Heaven—then rising with a smile,

Said, " We have watch'd, I and this old man here,

" Hour after hour, through the long lingering night,

" And now 'tis almost morning: I will stay

" Till I have heard my brother's distant horn

" From the west-woods;—but YOU are weary, youth?"

   " Oh, no! I will keep watch with you till dawn—

" To me most soothing is an hour like this!

" And who that saw, as now, the morning stars

" Begin to pale, and the gray twilight steal

" So calmly on the seas, and wide-hush'd world,

" Could deem there was a sound of misery

" On earth? nay, who could hear thy gentle voice,

" Fair maid, and think there was a voice of hate

" Or strife beneath the stillness of that cope

" Above us?   Oh! I hate the noise of arms—

" Here will I watch with you"—Then, after pause,

" Poor ENGLAND is not what it once has been;

" And strange are both our fortunes."

" ATHELING,"

(ADELA answer'd) " early piety

" Hath disciplin'd my heart to ev'ry change.

" How didst thou pass in safety from this land

" Of slavery and sorrow?"

He replied—

" When darker jealousy and lowering hate

" Sat on the brow of WILLIAM, England mourn'd,

" And one dark spirit of conspiracy

c

" Mutter'd its curses through the land.   'Twas then,

" With fiercer glare, the lion's eye was turn'd

" On me—My sisters and myself embark'd—

" The wide world was before us—we embark'd,

" With some few faithful friends, and from the sea

" Gazed tearful, for a moment, on the shores

" We left for ever—(so it then appear'd).

" Poor Margaret hid her face; but the fresh wind

" Swell'd the full mainsail, and the lessening land,

" The tow'rs, the spires, the villages, the smoke,

" Were seen no more.

                              " When now at sea, the winds

" Blew adverse, for to HOLLAND was our course—

" More fearful rose the storm—the east-wind sung

" Louder, till wreck'd upon the shores of Forth

" Our vessel lay—Here, friendless, we implored

" A short sojourn and succour—SCOTLAND's king

" Then sat in DUMFERMLINE—he heard the tale

" Of our distress—he flew himself to save—

" But when he saw my sister Margaret,

" Young, innocent, and beautiful in tears,

" His heart was mov'd.

     " 'Oh! welcome here,' he cried :

" ' 'Tis Heaven hath led you—Lady, look on me—

" ' If such a flower be cast to the bleak winds,

" ' 'Twere meet I took and wore it next my heart.'—

" Judg'd he not well, fair maid?

     " Thou know'st the rest—

" Compassion nurtur'd love, and Margaret

" (Such are the events of ruling Providence)

" Is now all Scotland's queen!

     " To join the bands

" Of warriors, in one cause assembled here,

" King Malcolm left his land of hills—his arm

" Might make the CONQUEROR tremble on his throne!

" E'en should we fail, my sister Margaret

" Would love and honour you ; and I might hope,

" (Oh! might I?) on the banks of Tay, or Tweed,

" With thee to wander, (where no curfew sounds,)

" And mark the summer-sun, beyond the hills,

       c 2

" Sink in its glory, and then, hand in hand,

" Wind through the woods, and——"

                                        Adela replied,

With smile complacent, " Listen—I will be

" (So to beguile the creeping hours of time)

" A tale-teller.—Two years we held sojourn

" In Denmark—two long weary years, and sigh'd,

" When, looking on the southern deep, we thought

" Of our poor country—' Give me men and ships!'

" Godwin still cried—' Oh! give me men and ships!'—

" The king commanded, and his armament—

" (A mightier never stemm'd the Baltic deep,

" Sent forth by sea-kings of the north, or bent

" On hardier enterprise: for NOT some isle

" Of the lone Orcades was now the prize,

" But ENGLAND's throne.)

                          " —His mighty armament

" Now left the shores of Denmark.   Our brave ships

" Burst through the Baltic straits, how gloriously!

" I heard the trumpets ring; I saw the sails

" Of nigh three hundred war-ships, the dim verge

" Of the remote horizon's skiey track

" Bestudding, here and there, like gems of light

".Dropt from the radiance of the morning sun

" On the gray waste of waters—So our ships

" Swept o'er the billows of the north, and steer'd

" Right on to ENGLAND.

                        " Foremost of the fleet

" Our gallant vessel rode—around the mast

" Emblazon'd shields were rang'd—and plumed crests

" Shook as the north-east rose—Upon the prow,

" More ardent, Godwin, my brave brother, stood,

" And milder Edmund, on whose mailed arm

" I hung, when the white waves before us swell'd,

" And parted.—The broad banner, in full length,

" Stream'd out its folds, on which the Saxon horse

" Ramp'd, as impatient on the land to leap,

" To which the winds still bore it bravely on ;

" Whilst the red cross, on the front banner, shone,

" The hoar deep crimsoning.

" Winds, bear us on—

" Bear us as cheerly, till white Albion's cliffs

" Resound to our triumphant shouts; till there,

" On his OWN TOW'R, that frowns above the Thames,

" Ev'n there we plant these BANNERS and this CROSS,

" And stamp the CONQUEROR and his CROWN to dust!—

" They would have kept me on a foreign shore,

" But could I leave my brothers? I with them

" Grew up, with them I left my native land,

" With them all perils have I braved, of sea,

" Or war, all storms of hard adversity:

" Let death betide, I reck not; all I ask,

" Is yet, once more in this sad world, to kneel

" UPON MY FATHER'S GRAVE, and kiss the earth.—

" When the fourth morning gleam'd along the deep,

" ' ENGLAND, OLD ENGLAND!' burst the general cry:

" ' ENGLAND, OLD ENGLAND!' Every eye, intent,

" Was turn'd; and Godwin pointed with his sword

" To Flamborough, pale rising o'er the surge:

" ' Nearer into the kingdom's heart bear on

" ' The death-storm of our vengeance !' Godwin cried.

" Soon, like a cloud, the Northern Foreland rose—

" Know ye those cliffs, tow'ring in giant state ?

" But hark ! along the shores alarum-bells

" Ring out more loud—trump answers trump—the swords

" Of hurrying horsemen, and projected spears,

" Flash to the sun—On yonder castle-walls

" A thousand bows are bent—Again, our course

" Back to the north is turn'd. Now twilight veil'd

" The sinking sands of Yarmouth, and we heard

" A long deep toll from many a village tow'r

" On shore—and lo ! the scatter'd in-land lights,

" That sprinkled, winding ocean's lowly verge,

" At once are lost in darkness—' GOD IN HEAVEN,

" ' IT IS THE CURFEW !' Godwin cried, and smote

" His forehead. We all heard that sullen sound

" For the first time, that night; but the winds blew—

" Our ship sail'd out of hearing; yet we thought

" Of the poor mother, who on winter nights,

" (When her belated husband from the wood

" Was not come back), her lonely taper lit,

" And turn'd the glass, and saw the faggot-flame

" Shine on the faces of her little ones—

" Those times will ne'er return.

                              " Darkness descends;

" Again the sun is rising o'er the waves:

" And now hoarse Humber roars beneath our keels,

" And we have landed——"

                              " Yea, and struck a blow,

" Such as may make the crowned Conqueror quail,"

Edgar replied.

                    " Grant, Heav'n, that we may live,"

Adela cried, " in love and peace again,

" When every storm is past—But this good man

" Is silent—Ailric, does no hope, e'en now,

" Arise on thy dark heart? Good father, speak,"

With aspect mild (on which its fitful light

The watch-tow'r lamp threw pale) the monk replied.

" Youth, on thy light hair, and ingenuous brow,

" Most comely sits the morn of life; on me,

" And this bare head, the night of time descends

" In sorrow.   I look back upon the past,

" And think of joy and sadness upon earth,

" Like the vast ocean's fluctuating toil

" From everlasting! I have seen its waste

" Now in the sunshine sleeping—now high-ridged

" With storms; and such the kingdoms of the earth.

" Yes, youth, and flattering fortune, and the light

" Of summer days, are as the radiance

" That flits along the solitary waves,

" E'en whilst we gaze, and say, ' how beautiful!'

" So fitful and so perishing the dream

" Of human things.   But there is light above,

" Undying; and, at times, faint harmonies

" Heard, by the weary pilgrim, in his way

" O'er perilous rocks, and through unwater'd wastes,

" Who looks up, fainting, and prays earnestly,

" To pass into that rest, whence sounds so sweet

" Come, whispering of hope; else it were best,

" Beneath the load the forlorn heart endures,

" To sink at once; to shut the eyes on things

" That sear the sight; and so to wrap the soul

" In sullen, tearless, ruthless apathy!

" Therefore, midst ev'ry human change, I drop

" A tear upon the cross, and all is calm;

" Yea, full of blissful—and of brightest views,

" On this dark tide of time.

                " Youth, thou hast known

" Adversity; even in thy morn of life,

" The spring-tide rainbow fades, and many days,

" And many years, perchance, of weal or woe

" Hang o'er thee: happy, if through ev'ry change

" Thy constant heart, thy stedfast view, be fix'd

" Upon that better kingdom, where the crown

" Immortal is held out to holy hope,

" Beyond the clouds that rest upon the grave.

  " Oh! I remember when King Harold stood

" Blooming in youth like thee: I saw him crown'd—

" I heard the loud voice of a nation hail

" His rising star: then, flaming in mid-heaven

" The red portentous comet, [6] like the hand

" Upon the wall, came forth: its fatal course

" All mark'd, and gazed in terror, as it look'd,

" With lurid light, upon this land. It pass'd—

" Old men had many bodings; but I saw,

" Reckless, King Harold, in his plumed helm,

" Ride foremost of the mailed chivalry,

" That, when the fierce Norwegian [7] pass'd the seas,

" Met his host, man to man; I saw the sword,

" Advanced and glittering, in the victor's hand,

" That smote the HARDRADA to the earth! To-day,

" King Harold rose, like an avenging God,

" To-morrow (so it seem'd, so short the space,)

" To-morrow, through the field of blood, we sought

" His mangled corse amid the heaps of slain—

" Shall I recount th' event more faithfully ?

" Its spectred memory never since that hour

" Has left my heart.

" WILLIAM was in his tent,

" Spread on the battle-plain, on that same night

" When seventy thousand dead lay at his feet—

" They, who at sun-rise, with bent bows and spears,

" Confronted and defied him, at his feet

" Lay dead!—alone, he watches in his tent,

" At midnight—midst a sight so terrible

" We came—we stood before him, where he sat,

" I and my brother Osgood.   ' Who are ye?'

" Stern he inquired; and Osgood thus replied.

" ' Conqueror, and Lord, and soon to be a King,

" ' We, two poor monks of Waltham Abbey, kneel

" ' Before thee, sorrowing! He who is slain

" ' To us was bountiful.   He raised those walls

" ' Where we devote our life to pray'r and praise.

" ' Oh! by the mercies which the God of all

" ' Hath shown to thee this day, grant our request;

" ' To search for his dead body, through this field

" ' Of terror, that his bones may rest with us.'

" ' Your king hath met the meed of broken faith,'

" William replied : ' But yet he shall not want

" ' A sepulchre ; and on this very spot

" ' My purpose stands, as I have vow'd to God,

" ' To build an holy monastery : here,

" ' A hundred monks shall pray for all who fell

" ' In this dread strife ; and YOUR KING HAROLD here

" ' Shall have due honours and a stately tomb.'

    " Still on our knees, we answer'd, ' Oh ! not so,

" ' Dread Sovereign ;—hear us, of your clemency.

" ' We beg his body ; beg it for the sake

" ' Of our successors ; beg it for ourselves,

" ' That we may bury it in the same spot

" ' Himself ordain'd when living ; where the choirs

" ' May sing for his repose, in distant years,

" ' When we are dust and ashes.'

                     " ' Then go forth,

" ' And search for him, at the first dawn of day,'

" King William said. We cross'd our breasts, and pass'd,

" Slow-rising, from his presence. So we went,

" In silence, to the quarry of the dead.

" The sun rose on that still and dismal host—

" Toiling from corse to corse, we trod in blood—

" From morn till noon toiling, and then I said,

" ' Seek Editha, her whom he loved.'   She came;

" And through the field of death she pass'd: she look'd

" On many a face, ghastly upturn'd; her hand

" Unloosed the helmet, smooth'd the clotted hair,

" And many livid hands she took in hers;

" Till stooping o'er a mangled corse, she shriek'd,

" Then into tears burst audibly, and turn'd

" Her face, and with a falt'ring voice pronounced,

" ' Oh! Harold!'   We took up, and bore the corse

" From that sad spot, and wash'd the ghastly wound

" Deep in the forehead, where the broken barb

" Was fix'd.

" So welt'ring from the field, we bore

" King Harold's corse.   A hundred Norman knights

" Met the sad train, with pikes that trail'd the ground.

" Our old men pray'd, and spoke of evil days

" To come; the women smote their breasts and wept;

" The little children knelt beside the way,

" As on to Waltham the funereal car

" Moved slow. Few and disconsolate the train

" Of English earls, for few, alas! remain'd,

" So many in the field of death lay cold.

" The horses slowly paced, till Waltham tow'rs

" Before us rose. THERE, with long taper'd blaze,

" Our brethren met us, chanting, two and two,

" The ' Miserere' of the dead. And THERE—

" But, my child Adela, you are in tears—

" There at the foot of the HIGH ALTAR lies

" The LAST OF SAXON KINGS.—Sad Editha,

" At distance, watch'd the rites, and from that hour

" We never saw her more."

                    A distant trump

Now rung—again! again!—and thrice a trump

Has answer'd from the walls of Ravenspur.

" My brothers! they are here!" Adela cried,

And left the tow'r in breathless ardour. " YORK

" Flames to the sky!" a general voice was heard—

The drawbridge clanks—into the inner court
A mailed man rides on—" York is no more!"
The cry without redoubles—On the ground
The rider flung his bloody sword, and raised
His helm dismounting—the first dawn of day
Gleam'd on the shatter'd plume.   " Oh! Adela,"
He cried, " your brother Godwin"—and she flew,
And murmuring, " my brave brother!" hid her face,
Clasping his mailed breast.   Soon gazing round,
She cried, " But where is Edmund ? Was he wont
" To linger ?"

                    " Edmund has a sacred charge,"
Godwin replied.   " But trust his anxious love,
" We soon shall hear his voice.   I need some rest—   "
" 'Tis now broad day ; but we have watch'd and fought :
" I can sleep sound, though the shrill bird of morn
" Mount and upbraid my slumbers with her song."

    Tranquil and clear the autumnal day declined:
The barks at anchor cast their lengthen'd shades
On the gray bastion'd walls; airs from the deep

Wander'd, and touch'd the cordage as they pass'd,

Then hover'd with expiring breath, and stirr'd

Scarce the quiescent pennant; the bright sea

Lay silent in its glorious amplitude,

Without; far up, in the pale atmosphere,

A white cloud, here and there, hung over-head,

And some red freckles streak'd the horizon's edge,

Far as the sight could reach : beneath the rocks,

That rear'd their dark brows beetling o'er the bay,

The gulls and guillemots, with short, quaint cry,

Just broke the sleeping stillness of the air,

Or skimming almost touch'd the level main,

With wings far seen, and more intensely white,

Opposed to the blue space; whilst Panope

Play'd in the offing. HUMBER's ocean-stream,

Inland, went sounding on, by rocks, and sands,

And castle, yet so sounding as it seem'd

A voice amidst the hush'd and listening world

That spoke of peace; whilst from the bastion's point

One piping red-breast might almost be heard.

D

Such quiet all things hush'd, so peaceable
The hour: the very swallows, ere they leave
The coast to pass a long and weary way
O'er ocean's solitude, seem to renew
Once more their summer feelings, as a light
So sweet would last for ever, whilst they flock
In the brief sunshine of the turret-top—

   'Twas at this hour of evening, Adela
And Godwin, now restored by rest, went forth,
Link'd arm in arm, upon the eastern beach,
Beyond the head-land's shade. If such an hour
Seem'd smiling on the heart, how smiled it now,
To him, who yesternight, a soldier, stood
Amid the direst sight of human strife,
And bloodshed; heard the cries, the trumpet's blast,
Ring o'er the dying; saw, with all its tow'rs,
A city blazing to the midnight sky,
And mangled groups of miserable men,
Gasping or dead, whilst with his iron heel

He splash'd the blood beneath!   How chang'd the scene!

The sun's last light upon the battlements,

The sea, the landscape, the peace-breathing air,

Remember'd both, of the departed hours

Of early life, when once they had A HOME,

A COUNTRY, where their father wore a crown.

What changes since that time, for them, and all

They loved! how many found an early grave,

Cut off by the red sword! how many mourn'd,

Scatter'd by various fates, through distant lands!

How desolate their own poor country, bound

By the Oppressor's chain! As thoughts like these

Arose, the bells of rural Nevilthorpe

Rung out a joyous peal, rung merrily,

For tidings heard from York: their melody

Mingled with things forgotten.   Adela

That instant turn'd to hide her tears, and saw

Her brother Edmund, leading by the hand

A boy of lovely mien, and footstep light,

Along the sands.   " My sister," Edmund cried,

" See, here, a foot-page I have brought from York,

" To serve a lady fair."   The boy held out

His hand to Adela, as he would say,

" Look, and protect me, lady."   Adela,

Advancing with a smile and glowing cheek,

Cried, " Welcome, truant brother," and then took

The child's right hand, and said, " My pretty page,

" And have you not a tale to tell to me?"

The boy spake nothing, but look'd earnestly

And anxiously at Edmund.   Edmund said,

" If he is silent, I must speak for him.

" 'Twas when the Minster flamed, and, sword in hand,

" Godwin, and Waltheof, and stern Hereward,

" Directed the red slaughter, black with smoke

" I burst into the citadel, and saw—

" Not the grim warder, with his huge axe up,

" But o'er her child a frantic mother, mute (9)

" With horror, in delirious agony,

" Clasping it to her bosom; stern and still

" The father stood, his hand upon his brow,

" As praying, in that hour, that God might make,

" In mercy, the last trial brief. ' FEAR NOT—

" ' I AM A MAN!—nay, fear not ME,' I cried,

" And seizing this child's hand, in safety placed,

" Amidst the smoke, and sounds and sights of death,

" Him and his mother! she with bursting heart

" Knelt down to bless me: when I saw that boy,

" So beautiful, I thought of Adela,

" And said, ' Oh! trust with his preserver this

" ' Your darling; for his safety, lo! I pledge

" ' My honour and my life.'

                           " And I have brought

" My trusted charge, that you, my Adela,

" May show him gentler courtesy than those,

" Whom war in its stern trade has almost steel'd."

   His sister kiss'd the child's light hair and cheek,

And folded his small hands in hers, and said,

" You shall be my true knight, and wear a plume,

" Wilt thou not, boy? and for a lady's love

" Fight, like a valiant soldier?"—" I will die,"

The poor child said, " for friends like those who saved

" My father and my mother;" and again

Adela kiss'd his forehead and his eyes,

And said, " But we are SAXONS!"

                    As she spoke,

The winds began to muster, and the sea

Swell'd with a sound more solemn, whilst the sun

Was sinking, and its last, and lurid light,

Streak'd the long line of cumbrous clouds, that hung

In wild red masses o'er the murmuring deep,

Now flick'ring fast with foam.   The sea-fowl flew

Rapidly on, o'er the black-lifted surge,

Borne down the wind, and then was seen no more.

Meantime the dark deep wilder heaves, and hark!

Heavily, over-head the gather'd storm

Comes sounding!

              Haste!—and in the castle-keep

List to the winds and waves that roar without.

The Grave of the last Saxon.

CANTO THE SECOND.

Waltham Forest—Tower—William and his Barons.

THERE had been fearful sounds in th' air last night
In the wild wolds of Holderness, when York
Flam'd to the midnight sky, and spells of death
Were heard amidst the depth of Waltham wood;
For there the wan and wëird sisters met
Their imps, and the dark spirits that rejoice
When foulest deeds are done on earth, and there
In dread accordance rose their dismal joy.

   " Around, around, around,

   " Troop and dance we to the sound,

   " Whilst mocking imps cry, Ho! ho! ho!

   " On earth there will be Woe! more woe!"

SPIRIT OF THE EARTHQUAKE.

Arise, swart Fiends, 'tis I command—
Burst your caves, and rock the land.

SPIRIT OF THE STORM.

Loud tempests, sweep the conscious wood!

SPIRIT OF THE BATTLE.

I scent from earth more blood! more blood!

SPIRIT OF THE FIRE.

When the wounded cry,
And the craven die,
I will ride on the spires,
And the red volumes of the bursting fires.

SPIRITS, AND NIGHT-HAGS.

" Around, around, around,
" Dance we to the dismal sound
" Of dying cries and mortal woe,
" Whilst mocking imps shout, Ho! ho! ho!"

Hear!

Spirits, that our hests perform

In the earthquake or the storm,

Appear, appear!

A fire is lighted—the pale smoke goes up:—

Obscure, terrific features through the clouds

Are seen, and a wild laughter heard, " We come!"

MINISTERING SPIRITS SING.

1.

I have syllables of dread;

They can wake the dreamless dead.

2.

I, a dark sepulchral song,

That can lead Hell's phantom-throng.

3.

Like a nightmare I will rest

This night upon KING WILLIAM's breast!

SPIRITS, AND NIGHT-HAGS.

" Around, around, around,

" Dance we to the dismal sound

" Of dying shrieks and mortal woe,

" Whilst antic imps shout, Ho! ho! ho!"

They vanish'd, and the earth shook where they stood.

That night, KING WILLIAM first, within the Tow'r,

Received his vassal Barons—in that Tow'r, (11)

Which oft since then has echo'd to night-shrieks

Of secret murder, or the lone lament—

Now other sounds were heard, for on this night

Its canopied and vaulted chambers rung

With minstrelsy; whilst sounds of long acclaim

Re-echoed, from the loop-holes, o'er the Thames:—

The drawbridge, and the pond'rous cullis-gate,

Frown'd on the moat—the flanking towers aspired

O'er the embattled walls, where proudly waved

The Norman banner. WILLIAM, laugh to scorn,

The murmurs of conspiracy and hate,

That round thee gather, like the storms of night

Mustering, when murder hides her visor'd mien!

Now, what hast Thou to fear? Let the fierce Dane

Into the centre of thy kingdom sweep,

With hostile armament, even like the tide

Of the hoarse Humber, on whose waves he rode!

Let foes confederate; let one voice of hate,

One cry of instant vengeance, one deep curse,

Be heard, from Waltham woods to Holderness!

Let Waltheof, stern in steel, let Hereward,

Impatient as undaunted, flash their swords;—

Let the boy Edgar, back'd by Scotland's King,

Advance his feeble claim, and don his casque,

Whose brows might better a blue bonnet grace;

Let Edwin and vindictive Morcar join

The sons of Harold! what hast thou to fear?

LONDON'S SOLE TOW'R might laugh their strength to scorn!

Upon that night, when YORK'S proud castle fell,

Here William held his court.   The torches glared
On crest or crozier.   Knights and prelates bow'd
Before THEIR SOVEREIGN.   He, his knights and peers
Surveying with a stern complacency,
Inclined not from his seat, o'ercanopied
With golden valance, woven by no hand,
Save of the Queen.   Yet calm his countenance
Shone, and his brow a dignified repose
Mark'd kingly; high his forehead, and besprent
With dark hair, interspersed with gray; his eye
Glanced amiable, chiefly when the light
Of a brief smile attemper'd majesty.
His beard was dark and heavy, yet diffused,
Low as the lion ramping on his breast.
Engrail'd upon the mail [12].

                        ODO approach'd,
And knelt, then rising, placed the diadem
Upon his brow, with laurels intertwined.
Again the voice of acclamation rung,
And from the galleries a hundred harps

Resounded ROLAND's song! " LONG LIVE the King!"

The barons, and the prelates, and the knights,

" Long live the Conqueror!" cried; " a God on earth!"

That instant the high vaulted chamber shook [13]

As with a blast from heaven, and all was mute

Around him, and the very fortress rock'd,

As it would topple on their heads: He rose

Disturb'd and frowning, for tumultuous thoughts

Crowded like night upon his heart; then waved

His hand!—The barons, abbots, knights, retire.

Behold him now alone! before a lamp

A crucifix appears; upon the ground

Lies the same sword that Hastings' battle dyed

Deep to the hilt in gore;—behold, he kneels

And prays, " Thou only, Lord, art great,—

" Have mercy on my sins!"   The crucifix

Shook as he spoke, shook visibly! and, hark!

There is a low moan, as of dying men,

At distance heard.

        Then William first knew fear [14].

He had heard tumults of the battle-field,

The noise, the glorious hurrahs, and the clang

Of trumpets round him, but no sound like this

Ere smote with unknown terror on his heart,

As if the eye of God that moment turn'd

And saw it beating.

                Rising slow, he flung

Upon a couch his agitated limbs:—

The lamp was near him; on the ground his sword

And helmet lay,—short troubled slumbers stole,

And darkly rose the spirit of his dream.

  He saw a field of blood,—it pass'd away;—

A glittering palace rose, with mailed men

Throng'd, and the voice of multitudes was heard

Acclaiming: suddenly the sounds were ceased,

The glittering palace vanish'd, and, behold,

Long winding cloisters, echoing to the chant

Of stoled fathers; and the mass-song ceased—

Then a dark tomb appear'd, and, lo! a shape

As of a phantom-king rose!

                    Nearer it came,

And nearer yet—in silence—through the gloom.

Advancing,—still advancing: the cold glare

Of armour shone as it approach'd, and now

It stands o'er William's couch!   The spectre gazed

Awhile, then lifting its dark visor up,

(Horrible vision!) show'd a grisly wound

Deep in its forehead, and therein appear'd

Gouts, as yet dropping from an arrow's point

Infix'd!   And that red arrow's deadly barb

The shadow drew, and pointed at the breast

Of William; and the blood dropp'd on his breast;

And through his steely arms one drop of blood

Came cold as death's own hand upon his heart!

Whilst a deep voice was heard, " Now sleep in peace,

" I am avenged!"

                    Starting, he exclaim'd,

" Hence, horrid phantom! Ho! Fitz-alain, ho!

" Montgomerie!"   Each baron, with a torch,

Before him stood!   " By dawn of day," he cried,

" We will to horse.   What passes in our thoughts

" We shall unfold hereafter.   By St. Anne,

" Albeit, not ten thousand phantoms sent

" By the dead Harold can divert our course,

" They may bear timely warning.

                            " 'Tis yet night—

" Give me a battle-song, ere daylight dawns;

" The song of Roland, or of Charlemagne!—

" Or our own fight at Hastings!—

                            " Torches!—ho!

" And let the gallery blaze with lights!   Awake,

" Harpers of Normandy, awake!   By Heav'n,

" I will not sleep till your full chords ring out

" The song of England's conquest!   Torches!—ho!"

   He spoke! again the blazing gallery

Echo'd the harpers' song.   Old Eustace led

The choir, and, whilst the king pac'd to and fro,

Thus rose the bold, exulting symphony.

SONG OF THE BATTLE OF HASTINGS.

1.

The Norman armament, beneath thy rocks St. Valerie,

Is moor'd; and, streaming to the morn, three hundred
banners fly;

Of crimson silk, with golden cross, effulgent o'er the rest,

That banner, proudest in the fleet, streams, which the
Lord had bless'd.

The gale is fair, the sails are set, cheerly the south wind
blows,

And Norman archers, all in steel, have grasp'd their good
yew-bows;

Aloud the harpers strike their harps, whilst morning light
is flung

Upon the cross-bows and the shields, that round the masts
are hung.

E

Speed on, ye brave, 'tis WILLIAM leads; bold Barons, at
    his word,
Lo! sixty thousand men of might for WILLIAM draw the
    sword.

2.

So, bound to England's southern shore, we roll'd upon
    the seas,
And gallant the white sails were set, and swelling to the
    breeze.
" On, on, to victory or death!" now rose the general cry;
The minstrels sung, " On, on, ye brave, to death or
    victory!"
Mark yonder ship, how straight she steers: ye knights
    and barons brave,
'Tis WILLIAM's ship, and proud she rides, the foremost
    o'er the wave.
And now we hail'd the English coast, and, lo! on Beachy
    Head,
The radiance of the setting sun majestical is shed.

The fleet sail'd on, till, Pevensey! we saw thy welcome
    strand;
Duke WILLIAM now his anchor casts, and dauntless leaps
    to land.

3.

The English host, by HAROLD led, at length appear in sight,
And now they raise a deafening shout, and stand prepar'd
    for fight;
The hostile legions halt awhile, and their long lines display,
Now front to front they stand, in still and terrible array.
Give out the word, " God, and our right!" rush like a
    storm along,
LIFT UP GOD'S BANNER, and advance, resounding Ro-
    LAND'S SONG!
Ye, spearmen, poise your lances well, by brave MONT-
    GOMERIE led,
Ye, archers, bend your bows, and draw the arrows to the
    head.
They draw—the bent bows ring—huzzah! another flight,
    and, hark!

How the sharp arrowy shower beneath the sun goes
    hissing dark.

Hark! louder grows the deadly strife, till all the battle-
    plain

Is red with blood, and heap'd around with men and horses
    slain.

On! Normans, on! DUKE WILLIAM cried, and, HAROLD,
    tremble Thou,

Now think upon thy perjury, and of thy broken vow.

The banner* of thy ARMED KNIGHT, thy shield, thy helm,
    are vain—

The fatal shaft has sped,—by Heav'n! it hisses in his
    brain!—

So William won the English crown, and all his foe-men
    beat,—

And Harold, and his Britons brave, lay silent at his feet.

" Enough! the day is breaking," cried the King :

" Away! away! be armed at my side,

" Without attendants, and to HORSE, to HORSE!

* Harold's banner had the device of an armed knight.

The Grave of the last Saxon.

CANTO THE THIRD.

Waltham Abbey and Forest—Wild Woman of the Woods.

AT WALTHAM ABBEY, o'er KING HAROLD'S GRAVE

A REQUIEM was chanted; for last night

A passing spirit shook the battlements,

And the pale monk, at midnight, as he watch'd

The lamp, beheld it tremble; whilst the shrines

Shook, as the deep foundations of the fane

Were mov'd. "Oh! pray for Harold's soul!" he cried.

And now, at matin bell, the monks were met,

And slowly pacing round the grave, they sung:

DIRGE.

1.

Peace, oh! peace be to the shade
Of him who here in earth is laid:
Saints, and spirits of the blest,
Look upon his bed of rest;
Forgive his sins, propitious be—
Dona pacem, Domine,
Dona pacem, Domine!

2.

When, from yonder window's height,
The moonbeams on the floor are bright,
Sounds of viewless harps shall die,
Sounds of Heaven's own harmony!
Forgive his sins, propitious be—
Dona pacem, Domine,
Dona pacem, Domine!

3.

By the spirits of the brave,

Who died the land they lov'd to save;

By the soldier's faint farewell,

By Freedom's blessing, where he fell;

Forgive his sins, propitious be—

Dona pacem, Domine.

Dona pacem, Domine!

4.

By a nation's mingled moan,

By Liberty's expiring groan,

By the saints, to whom 'tis given

To bear that parting groan to Heaven;

To his shade propitious be—

Dona pacem, Domine,

Dona pacem, Domine!

5

The PROUD and MIGHTY———

As they sung, the doors
Of the west portal, with a sound that shook
The vaulted roofs, burst open; and, behold!
An armed Norman knight, the helmet clos'd
Upon his visage, but of stature tall,
His coal-black armour clanking as he trod,
Advancing up the middle aisle alone,
Approach'd: he gaz'd in silence on the GRAVE
OF THE LAST SAXON; there awhile he stood,
Then knelt a moment, muttering a brief prayer:
The fathers cross'd their breasts—the mass-song ceas'd:—
Heedless of all around, the mailed man
Rose up, nor speaking, nor inclining, pac'd
Back through the sounding aisle, and left the fane.
The monks their interrupted song renew'd:

The proud and mighty, when they die,
With the crawling worm shall lie;
But who would not A CROWN resign,
HAROLD, for a rest like thine?

Saviour Lord, propitious be—
Dona pacem, Domine,
Dona pacem, Domine!

" Pacem" (as slow the stoled train retire),
" Pacem," the shrines and fretted roofs return'd.

'Twas told, three Norman knights, in armour, spurr'd
Their foaming steeds to the West Abbey door;
But who it was, that with his visor clos'd
Pass'd up the long and echoing fane alone,
And knelt on Harold's grave-stone, none could tell!
The stranger knights in silence left the fane,
And soon were lost in the surrounding shades
Of Waltham forest.
                    He, who foremost rode,
Pass'd his companions, on his fleeter steed,
And, muttering in a dark and dreamy mood,
Spurr'd on alone, till, looking round, he heard
Only the murmur of the woods above,

Whilst soon all traces of a road were lost
In the inextricable maze.   From morn
Till eve, in the wild woods he wander'd lost.
Night follow'd, and the gathering storm was heard
Among the branches.   List! there is no sound
Of horn far off, or tramp of toiling steed,
Or call of some belated forester;
No lonely taper lights the waste; the woods
Wave high their melancholy boughs, and bend
Beneath the rising tempest.   Heard ye not
Low thunder to the north?   The solemn roll
Redoubles through the dark'ning forest deep,
That sounds through all its solitude, and rocks,
As the long peal at distance rolls away.
Hark! the loud thunder crashes overhead,
And, as the red fire flings a fitful glare,
The branches of old oaks, and mossy trunks,
Distinct and visible shine out; and lo!
Interminable woods a moment seen,
Then lost again in deeper, lonelier night.

The torrent rain o'er the vast leafy cope

Comes sounding, and the drops fall heavily

Where the strange knight is shelter'd by the trunk

Of a huge oak, whose dripping branches sweep

Far round. Oh! happy, if beneath the flash

Some castle's banner'd battlements were seen,

Where the lone minstrel, as the storm of night

Blew loud without, beside the blazing hearth

Might dry his hoary locks, and strike his harp

(The fire relumin'd in his aged eyes)

To songs of Charlemagne!

                  Or, happier yet,

If some gray convent's bell remote proclaim'd

The hour of midnight service, when the chant

Was up, and the long range of windows shone

Far off, on the lone woods, whilst Charity

Might bless and welcome, in a night like this,

The veriest outcast! ANGEL OF THE STORM!

Ha! thy red bolt this instant shiv'ring rives

That blasted oak!

The horse starts back, and bounds
From the knight's grasp.   The way is dark and wild—
So dark and wild, as if the solitude
Had never heard the sound of human steps.
Pond'ring he stood, when by the lightning's glance
The knight now mark'd a small and craggy path.
Descending through the woody labyrinth,
He track'd his way slowly from brake to brake,
Till now he gain'd a deep sequester'd glen—
" I fear not storms, nor thunders, nor the sword,"
The knight exclaim'd : " that eye alone I fear!
" God's stern and stedfast eye upon the heart !
" Yet peace is in the grave where HAROLD sleeps."

" Who speaks of Harold ?" cried a woman's voice,
Heard through the deep night of the woods—" HE spoke,"
A stern voice answer'd, " HE, of Harold spoke,
" Who fear'd his sword in the red front of war,
" Less than the powers of darkness :" and he cross'd
His breast, for at that instant rose the thought

Of the weird sisters of the wold, that mock

Night wanderers, and " syllable men's names"

In savage solitude—" If now," he cried,

" Dark minister, thy spells of wizard power

" Have rais'd the storm and wild winds up, APPEAR !"

He scarce had spoken, when, by the red flash

That glanc'd along the glen, half visible

Appear'd a tall, majestic female form ;

So visible, her eyes' intenser light

Shone wildly through the darkness ; and her face,

On which one pale flash more directly shone,

Was like a ghost's by moonlight, as she stood

A moment seen : her lips appear'd to move

Muttering, whilst her long locks of ebon hair

Stream'd o'er her forehead, by the bleak winds blown

Upon her heaving breast.

                The knight advanc'd—

Th' expiring embers from a cave within,

Now waken'd by the night-air, shot a light,

Fitful and trembling, and this human form,

If it was human, at the entrance stood,

As seem'd, of a rude cave.   You might have thought

She had strange spells, such a mysterious power

Was round her, such terrific solitude,

Such night, as of the kingdom of the grave,

Whilst hurricanes seem'd to obey her hest.

And she no less admired, when, front to front,

By the rekindling ember's darted gleam,

A mailed man, of proud illustrious port,

She mark'd; and thus, but with unfaltering voice,

She spake—

    " Yes! it was HAROLD's name I heard!

" Whence, and what art thou? I have watch'd the night,

" And listen'd to the tempest as it howl'd,

" And whilst I listening lay, methought I heard,

" Even now, the tramp as of a rushing steed—

" Therefore I rose, and look'd into the dark,

" And now I hear one speak of Harold: say,

" Whence, and what art thou, solitary man?

" If lost and weary, enter this poor shed—

" If wretched, pray with me—if on dark deeds

" Intent, I am a most poor woman, cast

" Into the depths of mortal misery!

" The desolate have nought to lose:—pass on!

" I had not spoken, but for Harold's name,

" By thee pronounc'd: it sounded in my ears

" As of a better world—ah, no! of days

" Of happiness in this.—Whence, who art THOU?"

" I am a NORMAN, woman; more to know

" Seek not:—and I have been to HAROLD'S GRAVE,

" Remembering the MIGHTIEST are but dust;

" And I have pray'd the peace of God might rest

" UPON HIS SOUL."

　　　　　　　　　" And, by our blessed Lord,

" The deed was holy," that lorn woman said;

" And may the benediction of all saints,

" Whoe'er thou art, rest on thy head.　But say,

" What perilous mischance hath hither led

" Thy footsteps in an hour and night like this?"

" Over his grave, of whom we spake, I heard

" The mass-song sung! I knelt upon his grave,

" And pray'd for my own sins! I left the fane,

" And heard the chanted rite at distance die.

" Returning through these forest shades, with thoughts

" Not of this world, I press'd my panting steed

" The foremost of the Norman knights, and pass'd

" The track, that, leading to the forest-ford,

' Winds through the opening thickets—on a height

' I stood and listened, but no voice replied—

" The storm descended: at the lightning's flash

" My good steed burst the reins, and frantic fled—

" I was alone: the small and craggy path

" Led to this solitary glen; and here,

" As dark and troubled thoughts arose, I mused

" Upon the dead man's sleep; FOR GOD, I thought,

" THIS NIGHT, SPOKE IN THE ROCKING OF THE WINDS!"

" There is a JUDGE in heaven," the woman said,

" Who seeth all things; and there is a VOICE,

" Inaudible midst the tumultuous world,

" That speaks of fear or comfort to the heart

" When all is still !   But shroud thee in this cave

" Till morning : such a sojourn may not please

" A courtly knight, like echoing halls of joy.

" I have but some wild roots, a bed of fern,

" And no companion save this bloodhound here,

" Who, at my beck, would tear thee to the earth—

" Yet enter—fear not"—And that poor abode

The proud knight enter'd, with rain-drenched plume.

" Yet here I dwell in peace," the woman said,

" Remote from towns, nor start at the dire sound

" Of that ACCURSED CURFEW !—Soldier-knight,

" Thou art a NORMAN !   Had th' invader spurn'd

" All charities in thy own native land,

" Yes—thou would'st know what injur'd Britons feel."

" Nay, ENGLISHWOMAN, thou dost wrong our king,"

The knight replied : " conspiracy and fraud

" Hourly surrounding him, at last compell'd

" Stern Rigour to awake.   What ! shall the bird

F

" Of thunder slumber on the citadel,

" And blench his eye of fire, when, looking down,

" He sees, in ceaseless enmity combin'd,

" Those who would pluck his feathers from his breast,

" And cast them to the winds?   Woman, on thee,

" Haply, the tempest of the times has beat

" Too roughly; but thy griefs HE can requite!'

   The indignant woman answer'd, " HE requite!

" Can he bring back the dead? Can he restore

" Joy to the broken-hearted? He requite!

" Can he pour plenty on the vales his frown

" Has blasted? bid sweet evening hear again

" The village pipe? and the fair flow'rs revive

" His bloody footstep crush'd?   For poverty,

" I reck it not: what is to me the night,

" Spent cheerless, and in gloom, and solitude?

" I fix my eye upon that crucifix,

" I mourn for those that are not—for my brave,

" My buried countrymen!—Of this no more!—

" Thou art a foe; but a brave soldier-knight

" Would scorn to wrong a woman; and if death

" Could arm my hand this moment, thou wert safe

" In a poor cottage as in royal halls.

" Here rest awhile till morning dawns—the way

" No mortal could retrace:—'twill not be long,

" And I can cheat the time with some old strain—

" For, Norman though thou art, thy soul has felt

" Ev'n as a man, when sacred sympathy

" This morning led thee to KING HAROLD'S GRAVE."

The woman sat beside the hearth, and stirr'd

The embers, or with fern or brushwood rais'd

A fitful flame, but cautious, lest its light

Some roving forester might mark.   At times,

The small and trembling blaze shone on her face,

Still beautiful, and show'd the dark eye's fire

Beneath her long black locks. When she stood up,

A dignity, though in the garb of want,

Seem'd round her, chiefly when the brush-wood-blaze

Glanc'd through the gloom, and touch'd the dusky mail
Of the strange knight—then—with sad smile she sung:

Oh! when 'tis Summer weather,
And the yellow bee, with fairy sound,
The waters clear is humming round,
And the cuckoo sings unseen,
And the leaves are waving green—
    Oh! then 'tis sweet,
    In some remote retreat,
To hear the murmuring dove,
With those whom on earth alone we love,
And to wind through the green-wood together.

But when 'tis Winter weather,
    And crosses grieve,
    And friends deceive,
    And rain and sleet
    The lattice beat—
    Oh! then 'tis sweet

To sit and sing

Of the friends, with whom, in the days of spring,

We roam'd through the green-wood together.

The bloodhound slept upon the hearth—he rais'd

His head, and, through the dusk, his eyes were seen,

Fiery, a moment; but again he slept,

When she her song renew'd.

        " Though thy words might well deceive me—

            That is pass'd—subdu'd I bend;

        Yet, for mercy, do not leave me

            To the world without a friend!

        Oh! thou art gone! and would, with thee,

            Remembrance too had fled!

        She lives to bid me weep, and see

            The wreath I cherish'd dead.

The knight, through the dim lattice, watch'd the clouds

Of morn, now slowly struggling in the cast,

When, with a voice more thrilling, and an air
Wilder, again a sad song she inton'd—

    " Upon the field of blood,
      Amidst the bleeding brave,
    O'er his pale corse I stood—
      But HE is in HIS GRAVE.
    I wip'd his gory brow,
      I smooth'd his clotted hair—
    But he is at peace, in the cold ground now—
      Oh! when shall WE meet there?"

At once, horns, trumpets, and the shouts of men,
Were heard above the valley.   At the sound,
The knight, upstarting from his dreamy trance,
High rais'd his vizor, and his bugle rung,
Answering.   " By God in heaven, thou ART THE KING!"
The woman said.   Again the clarions rung—
Like lightning! Alain and Montgomerie
Spurr'd through the wood, and led a harness'd steed

To the lone cabin's entrance, whilst the train

Sent up a deaf'ning shout, " Long live the King !"

He, ere he vaulted to the saddle-bow,

Turn'd with a look benevolent, and cried,

" Barons and lords, to this poor woman here

" Haply I owe my life ! Let HER NOT NEED !"

   " Away !" she cried, " KING OF THESE REALMS, away !

" I ask not wealth nor pity—least from THEE,

" Of all men."   As the day began to dawn,

More fix'd and dreadful seem'd her stedfast look,

The long black hair upon her labouring breast

Stream'd, whilst her neck, as in disdain, she rais'd

Swelling—her eyes a wild terrific light

Shot, and her voice, with intonation deep,

Utter'd a curse, that ev'n the bloodhound crouch'd

Beneath her feet, whilst with stern look she spoke :—

" Yes ! I AM EDITHA ! SHE whom he lov'd—

" SHE, whom thy sword has left in solitude,

" How desolate ! yes—I AM EDITHA !—

" AND THOU HAST BEEN TO HAROLD'S GRAVE—oh ! think,

" KING, WHERE THY OWN WILL BE! HE rests in peace;

" But ev'n a spot is to thy bones denied—

" I see thy carcass trodden under foot——

" THY CHILDREN—HIS, with filial reverence,

" Still think upon the spot where he is laid,

" Though distant and far-sever'd—But thy son*,

" Thy eldest born, ah! see, he lifts the sword

" Against his father's breast!—Hark, hark! the chase

" Is up! in that wild forest thou hast made!—

" The deer is flying—the loud horn resounds—

" Hurrah! the arrow that laid HAROLD low—

" It flies—it trembles in the RED KING'S HEART †!

" NORMAN, HEAV'N'S HAND IS ON THEE, and THE CURSE

" Of this devoted land! HENCE, TO THY THRONE!"—

The King a moment with compassion gaz'd,

And now the clarions, and the horns, and trumps

Rung louder; the bright banners in the winds

Wav'd beautiful; the neighing steeds aloft

---

* Robert of Normandy.   † William Rufus, called the Red King.

Mantled their manes, and up the valley flew,

And soon have left behind, the glen, the cave.

Of solitary Editha, and sounds

Of her last agony!

                    " Montgomerie,"

King William, turning, cried, " when this whole land

" Is portion'd (for till then we may not hope

" For lasting peace) FORGET NOT EDITHA * !"

   In the gray beam the spires of London shone,

And the proud banner on the bastion

Of William's Tower was seen above the Thames,

As the gay train, slow winding through the woods,

Approach'd ; when, lo! with spurs of blood, and voice

Falt'ring, upon a steed, whose lab'ring chest

Heav'd, and whose bit was wet with blood and froth,

A courier met them.

* It is a singular fact, that the name of Editha Pulcherrima occurs in Domesday.—See Turner.

" York!—oh King!" he cried,
" York is in ashes!—all thy Normans slain!"

" Now, by the splendour of the throne of God !"
King William cried, " nor woman, man, nor child,
" Shall live."—Terrific flash'd his eye of fire,
And darker grew his frown; then, looking up,
He drew his sword, and with a vow to Heav'n,
Amid his barons, to the trumpet's clang
Rode onward (breathing vengeance) to the Tow'r!

The Grave of the last Saxon.

CANTO THE FOURTH.

Wilds of Holderness—Hags—Parting on the Humber—
Waltham Abbey, and Grave—Conclusion.

THE moon was high—when, mid the wildest wolds
Of Holderness, where erst that structure vast,
An idol-temple *, in old heathen times
Frown'd, with gigantic shadow to the moon,
That oft had heard the dark song, and the groans
Of midnight sacrifice—

     There, the wan sisters met,—
They circled the rude stone, and call'd the dead,
And sung by turns their more terrific song:

 * This temple Camden places at Delgovitia.

FIRST HAG.

I look'd in the seer's prophetic glass,
And saw the deeds that should come to pass—
From Carlisle-Wall to Flamborough Head,
The reeking soil was heap'd with dead.

SECOND HAG.

The towns were stirring at dawn of day,
And the children went out in the morn to play;
The lark was singing on holt and hill—
I look'd again, but the towns were still,
The murder'd child on the ground was thrown,
And the lark was singing to heav'n alone.

THIRD HAG.

I saw a famish'd mother lie,
Her lips were livid, and glaz'd her eye;
The tempest was rising, and sung in the south,
And I snatch'd the blade of grass from her moutl

FOURTH HAG.

By the rolling of the drums!
Hitherward KING WILLIAM comes:
The night is struggling with the day—
Hags of darkness! hence! away!

WILLIAM is in the north—the avenging sword
Descended like a whirlwind where he pass'd—
Slaughter and Famine at his bidding wait,
Like lank, impatient bloodhounds, till he cries
" Pursue!" Again the Norman banner floats
Triumphant on the citadel of York,
Where, circled with the blazonry of arms,
Amid his Barons, WILLIAM holds his state.
The boy preserv'd from death, young MALET, kneels,
With folded hands:—His father, mother kneel,
Imploring clemency for HAROLD's sons—
For Edmund most. Bareheaded Waltheof bends,
And yields the keys!—A breathless courier came;
" What tidings?"—" O'er the seas the Danes are fled—
" Morcar and Edwin in Northumberland,

" Amidst its wildest mountains, seek to hide

" Their broken hopes—their troops are all dispers'd.

" Malcolm alone, and the boy Atheling,

" And the two sons of the dead Harold, wait

" The winds to bear them to the North away."—

" Bid forth a thousand spearmen," William cried:

" Now, by the resurrection, and the throne

" Of God, King Malcolm shall repent the hour

" He ere drew sword in England!—Hence, away!"

The west wind blows—the boat is on the beach,

The clansmen are embark'd—the pipe is heard—

Whilst thoughtful Malcolm and young Atheling

Linger the last upon the shore: and there

Are Harold's children, the gray-headed monk,

Godwin, and Edmund, and poor Adela:—

Then Malcolm spoke—" The lot is cast: oh! fly

" From this devoted land, and live with us,

" Amidst our lakes and mountains!"—" Adela,"

Atheling whisper'd, " does thy heart say Yes?

" For in this world we ne'er may meet again."

" The brief hour calls—come, Adela," exclaim'd
Malcolm, and kindly took her hand.   She look'd
To heaven, and fell upon her knees—then rose,
And answer'd:

     ' " Sire, when my brave father fell,
" We three were exiles on a distant shore,
" And never, or in solitude or courts,
" Was God forgotten—all is in his hand.
" When those whom I had lov'd from infancy
" Here join'd the din of arms, I came with them—
" With them I have partaken good and ill,
" Have in the self-same mother's lap been laid,
" The same eye gaz'd on us with tenderness,
" And the same mother pray'd prosperity
" Might still be ours through life!   Alas! our lot,
" How different!

     " Yet let THEM go with you,
" I argue not—the first time in our lives,
" If it be so, we here shall separate—
" Whatever fate betide, I will not go

" Till I have knelt upon MY FATHER'S GRAVE!"—

" 'Tis perilous to think," Atheling cried,

" Most perilous—how 'scape the Norman's eye?"—

She turn'd, and with a solemn calmness said,

" If we should perish—at the hour of death

" My father will look down from Heaven, and say,

" ' Come, my poor child!—Oh! come where I am bless'd!'

" My brothers, seek your safety—Here I stand

" Resolv'd—and never will I leave these shores

" Till I have knelt upon MY FATHER'S GRAVE!"—

" We never will forsake thee!" Godwin cried.

" Let death betide!" said Edmund, " we will go—

" Yes! go with thee, or perish!"

                              As he spoke,

The pilot gave the signal—" Then farewell!"

King Malcolm cried, " friends lately met, and now

" To part for ever!" and he kiss'd the cheek

Of Adela, and took brave Godwin's hand

And Edmund's, and then said, almost in tears,

" It is not now too late! 'yet o'er my grave

" So might a duteous daughter weep !"   " God speed
" Brave Malcolm to his father's land !" they cried.
The ships, beyond the promontory's point,
Were anchor'd—and the tide was ebbing fast.

    Then Ailric—" Sire, not unforeseen by me
" Was this sad day :—Oh ! King of Scotland, hear—
" I was a brother of that holy house
" Where Harold's bones are buried—from my vows
" I was absolv'd, and follow'd—for I lov'd
" His children—follow'd them through every fate.
" My few gray hairs will soon descend in peace,
" When I shall be forgotten ; but till THEN,
" My services, my last poor services,
" To THEM I have devoted, for the sake
" Of HIM, their father, and MY KING, to whom,
" All, in this world, I ow'd ! Protect them, Lord,
" And bless them, when the turf is on my head,
" And, in their old age, may they sometimes think
" Of Ailric, cold and shrouded in his grave,

G

" When summer smiles.—Sire, listen, whilst I pray

" One boon of thy compassion; NOT for me—

" I reck not whether vengeance wake or sleep—

" But for the safety of this innocent maid

" I speak.   South of the Humber, in a cave,

" Conceal'd amidst the rocks and tangled brakes,

" I have deposited some needful weeds

" For this sad hour,—For well, indeed, I knew,

" If all should fail, this maiden's last resolve,

" To KNEEL UPON HER FATHER'S GRAVE, OR DIE.

" For this I have provided : but the time

" Is precious, and the sun is west'ring slow :

" The fierce eye of the lion may be turn'd

" Upon this spot to-morrow ! Adela,

" Now, hear your friend, your father ! the fleet hour

" Is passing, never to return : Oh ! seize

" The instant.—Thou, King Malcolm, grant my pray'r !—

" If we embark, and leave the shores this night,

" The voice of fame will bruit it far and wide,

" That Harold's children fled with thee, and sought

" A refuge in thy kingdom—None will know

" Our destination—In thy boat convey'd,

" We may be landed near the rocky cave,—

" The boat again ply to thy ships, and they

" Plough homeward the north seas, whilst WE ARE left

" To FATE!"—Again the pilot's voice was heard—

And, o'er the sand-hills, an approaching file

Of Norman soldiers, with projected spears,

Already seem'd as rushing on their prey.

Then Ailric took the hand of Adela—

She and her brothers, and young Atheling,

And Scotland's king, are in one boat embark'd—

Meantime the sun sets red, and twilight shades

The sinking hills—The solitary boat

Has reach'd the adverse shore.

                    " Here, then, we part!"

King Malcolm said; and every voice replied,

" God speed brave Malcolm to his father's land!"

Ailric, the brothers, and their sister, left

The boat—they stood upon the moonlight beach,
Still list'ning to the sounds, as they grew faint,
Of the receding oars, and watching still
If one white streak at distance, as they dipp'd,
Were seen, till all was solitude around.
Pensive, they sought a refuge for that night
In the bleak ocean-cave.—The morning dawns,
The brothers have put off the plumes of war,
Dropping one tear upon the sword!   Disguis'd
In garb to suit their fortunes, they appear
Like shipwreck'd seamen of Armorica,
By a Franciscan hermit through the land
Led to St. Alban's shrine, to offer vows—
Vows to the God, who heard them in that hour,
When all besides had perish'd in the storm.

Wreck'd near his ocean-cave, an eremite
(So went the tale of their disastrous fate)
Sustain'd them, and now guides them through a land
Of strangers—That fair boy was wont to sing

Upon the mast, when the still ship went slow
Along the seas, in sunshine—and that garb
Conceals the lovely, light-hair'd Adela.
The cuckoo's note in the deep woods was heard
When forth they far'd.   At many a convent gate
They stood and pray'd for shelter, and their pace
Hasten'd, if high amid the clouds they mark'd
Some solitary castle lift its brow
Gray in the distance—hasten'd, so to reach,
Ere it grew dark, its hospitable tow'rs—
There the lithe minstrel sung his roundelay.

Listen, lords and ladies bright:
I can sing of many a knight
Who fought in paynim lands afar—
Of Bevis, or of Iscapar.
I have tales of wand'ring maids,
And fairy elves in haunted glades,
Of phantom-troops that silent ride
By the moonlight forest's side.

I have songs (fair maidens, hear !)
To warm the love-lorn lady's ear—
The choice of all my treasures take,
And grant us food for pity's sake.

When tir'd, at noon, by the white waterfall,
In some romantic and secluded glen,
They sat, and heard the blackbird overhead
Singing, unseen, a song, such as they heard
In infancy.—* So every vernal morn
Brought with it smell of flowers, or song of birds,
Mingled with many shapings of old things,
And days gone by !—Then up again, to scale
The airy mountain, and behold the plain
Stretching below, and fading far away,
How beautiful ! yet still to feel a tear
Starting (even when it shone most beautiful),
To think, " HEBE, in the country of our birth,

* William took the field in spring.

" No rest is ours!"

                " ON, TO OUR FATHER'S GRAVE!"

So southward through the country they had pass'd

Now many days, and casual shelter found,

In villages, or hermit's lonely cave,

Or castle, high-embattled on the point

Of some steep mountain, or in convent walls;

For most with pity heard his song, and mark'd

The countenance of the way-faring boy;

Or when the pale monk, with his folded hands

Upon his breast, pray'd, " For the love of God,

" Pity the poor," gave alms, and bade them " Speed!"

And now, in distant light, the pinnacles

Of a gray fane appear'd, whilst on the woods

Still evening shed its parting light:—" Oh! say—

" Say, villager, what tow'rs are those that rise

" Eastward beyond the alders?"

                    " Know ye not,"

He answer'd, " WALTHAM ABBEY? HAROLD there

" Is buried—He, who in the fight was slain

" At HASTINGS!"—To the cheek of Adela
A deadly paleness came.   " On—let us on,"
Faintly she cried, and held her brother's arm,
And hid her face a moment with her hand!
And now the massy portal's sculptur'd arch
Before them rose.

    " Say, porter," Ailric cried,
" Poor mariners, wreck'd on the northern shores,
" Ask charity!—Does aged Osgood live?
" Tell him a poor Franciscan, wand'ring far,
" And wearied, for the love of God would ask
" His charity."

    Osgood came slowly forth—
The light that touch'd the western turret, fell
On his pale face.   The pilgrim-father said,
" I am your brother Ailric—look on me!
" And THESE ARE HAROLD'S CHILDREN!"

      Whilst he spoke,
Godwin, advancing, with emotion cried,
" We are his children! I am Godwin, this

" Is Edmund, and lo! poor and in disguise,

" Our sister!—we would KNEEL UPON HIS GRAVE—

" OUR FATHER'S!"

                    " Come yet nearer," Osgood said,

" Yet nearer!" and that instant Adela

Look'd up, and wiping from the lids a tear,

" Have you forgotten Adela?"

                              " Oh God!"

The old man trembling cried, " ye are indeed

" Our benefactor's children! Adela,

" Edmund, brave Godwin! welcome to these walls—

" Welcome, my old companion!" and he fell

Upon the neck of Ailric, and both wept.

Then Osgood—" Children of that honour'd lord

" Who gave us all, go near and bless his grave."

One parting sunbeam yet upon the floor

Rested—it pass'd away, and darker gloom

Was gathering in the aisles. Each footstep's sound

Was more distinctly heard, for all beside

Was silent. Slow along the glimmering fane

They pass'd, like shadows risen from the tombs.

The entrance-door was clos'd, lest ought intrude

Upon the sanctity of this sad hour!

The inner quoir they enter, part in shade

And part in light, for now the rising moon

Began to glance upon the shrines, and tombs,

And pillars : trembling through the windows high

One beam, a moment, on that cold gray stone

Is flung—the word " Infelix" * is scarce seen—

" BEHOLD HIS GRAVE-STONE!" Osgood said.   Each eye

Was turn'd.   Awhile intent they gaz'd, then knelt

Before the altar, on the marble stone!

No sound was heard through all the dim expanse

Of the vast building, none but of the air

That came in dying echoes up the aisle,

Like whispers heard at the confession-chair.

Thus Harold's children, hand in hand, knelt down—

Upon THEIR FATHER'S GRAVE KNELT down! and pray'd—

* In some accounts it is said the only inscription on the tomb was
" Infelix Harold."

" Have mercy on his soul—HAVE MERCY, LORD!"

They knelt a lengthen'd space, and bow'd their heads,

Some natural tears they shed, and cross'd their breasts,

Then, rising slowly up, look'd round, and saw

A monk approaching near, unmark'd before;

And in the farther distance the tall form

As of a female.   He who wore the hood

And habit of a monk, approach'd and spoke—

" Brothers! beloved sister! know ye not

" These features?"—and he rais'd his hood—" Behold

" Me—me, your brother Marcus! whom these weeds,

" Since last we met, have hid from all the world:

" Let ME kneel with you HERE!"

> When Adela

Beheld him, she exclaim'd, " Oh! do we meet

" Here, my lost brother, o'er a father's grave?

" You live, restor'd a moment in this world,

" To us as from the grave!"   And Godwin took

His hand, and said, " My brother, tell us all—

" How have you liv'd unknown?—Oh! tell us all."

" When in that grave our father (he replied)

" Was laid, ye fled, and I in this sad land

" Remain'd to cope with fortune. To these walls

" I came, when Ailric, from his vows absolv'd,

" With you was wand'ring. None my lineage knew,

" Or name, but I, some time, had won regard

" From the Superior—Osgood knew me not,

" For with Earl Edwin I had liv'd from youth—

" To our Superior thus I knelt and pray'd:

" ' Sir, I beseech you, for the love of God,

" ' And of our Lady Mary, and St. John,

" ' You would receive me here to live and die

" ' Among you.'—What most mov'd my heart to take

" The vows, was this, that here, from day to day,

" From year to year, within the walls he rais'd,

" I might behold my Father's grave! This eve

" I sat in the Confessional, unseen,

" When you approach'd—I scarce restrain'd the tear,

" From many recollections, when I heard

" A tale of sorrow and of sin! Come near,

" WOMAN of woe!"—and a wan woman stood

Before them, tall and stately; her dark eyes

Shone, as th' uncertain lamp cast a brief glare,

And show'd her neck, and raven hair, and lips

Moving—She spoke not, but advanc'd and knelt—

She, too—on HAROLD's GRAVE; then pray'd aloud,

" OH! GOD BE MERCIFUL TO HIM—AND ME!"

  " Who art thou?" Godwin cried.

                    " Ah! know ye not

" The wretched EDITHA? No CHILDREN's LOVE

" Could equal MINE!—I trod among the dead!

" Did I not, fathers?—trod among the dead

" From corse to corse, or saw men's dying eyes

" Fix'd upon mine, and heard such groans as yet

" Rive, with remembrance, my torn heart—I found

" HIM, who rests here, where then he lay in blood!

" When he was buried, I beheld the rites

" At distance, and with broken heart retir'd

" To the wild woods; there I have liv'd unseen

" From that sad hour. Late, when the tempest rock'd,

" At midnight, a proud soldier shelter sought

" In my lone cell; 'twas when the storm was heard

" Through the deep forest, and he too had knelt

" At HAROLD's grave!—Who was it?—HE! the KING!

" Say, fathers, was it not the hand of God

" That led his footsteps there! —But has he learn'd

" Humility? oh! ask this bleeding land.

" Last night, a phantom came to me in dreams,

" And a voice said, ' Come, visit my cold grave!'

" I came, by some mysterious impulse led;

" I heard the even-song, and when the sound

" Had ceas'd, and all departed, save one monk,

" Who stood and gaz'd upon this grave alone,

" I pray'd that he would hear me, at this hour,

" Confess my secret sins, for my full heart

" Was labouring.   It was Harold's son who sat

" In the Confessional, to me unknown—

" But all is now reveal'd—and lo! I stand

" Before you!"

   As she spoke, a thrilling awe

Came to each heart: loftier she seem'd to stand

In the dim moonlight; sorrowful, yet stern,

Her aspect; and her breast was seen to beat:

Her eyes were fix'd, and shone with fearful light—

She rais'd her right hand, and her dark hair fell

Upon her neck, whilst all, scarce breathing, heard:

" My spirit labours!" she exclaim'd! " this night!

" The tomb! the altar! Ha! the vision strains

" My senses to oppression!   Mark'd ye not

" The trodden throne restor'd? the Saxon line*

" Of England's monarchs bursting through the gloom?

" Lady, I look on thee—In distant years,

" Ev'n from the Northern throne which thou shalt share, †

" A warrior-monarch shall arise, whose arm,

" In concert with this country, now bow'd low,

" Shall tear the EAGLE from a CONQUEROR's grasp,

" Far greater than THIS NORMAN!

* The Saxon line was restored through the sister of Atheling.

† A daughter of Harold married Waldimir of Russia. This part was
written when the Emperor of Russia was in England.

"Spare, oh God!—

"My burning brain!"—Then, with a shriek, she fell

Insensible upon the SAXON's GRAVE!

They bore her from the fane—and Godwin said,

"Peace, peace be with her, now and evermore!"

He, taking Marcus by the hand, "Yet, here

"Thou shalt behold—behold, from day to day,

"This HONOUR'D GRAVE! But where in the great world

"Shall be thy place of rest, poor Adela?"—

"Oh! God be ever with her!" Marcus cried,

"With her, and you, my brothers! Here we part,

"Never to meet again—whate'er your fate,

"I shall remember with a brother's love,

"And pray for you! but all my spirit rests

"In other worlds—in worlds, oh! not like THIS!

"Ye may return to this sad scene when I

"Am dust and ashes; ye may yet return—

"And visit this sad spot; perhaps when age

"Or grief has brought such change of heart as now

"I feel, then shall you look upon MY grave—

" And shed one tear for HIM, whose latest pray'r

" Will be—Oh! bless you! bless MY SISTER, Lord!"

Then Adela, with lifted look compos'd,—

" FATHER, IT IS PERFORM'D,—the duty vow'd

" When we return'd to this devoted land,

" The last sad duty of a daughter's love!—

" And now I go in peace—go to a world

" Of sorrow, conscious that a father's voice

" Speaks to my soul, and that thine eye, oh God,

" Whate'er the fortunes of our future days,

" Is o'er us.   THOU, DIRECT OUR ONWARD ROAD!"

O'er the LAST SAXON'S GRAVE, old Osgood rais'd

His hands, and pray'd—

          " FATHER OF HEAV'N AND EARTH!

" All is beneath thine eye! 'tis ours to bend

" In silence.   Children of misfortune, lov'd,

" Rever'd—children of HIM who rais'd these roofs,

" No home is found for YOU in this sad land;

" And none, perhaps, may know the spot, or shed

" A tear upon the earth where ye are laid!"

So saying, on their heads he plac'd his hands,

H

And bless'd them all—but, after pause, rejoin'd,

" 'Tis dangerous lingering here—the fire-ey'd Lynx

" Would lap your blood!—Westward, beyond the Lea,

" There is a cell, where ye may rest to-night."

   The portal open'd—on the battlements

The moonlight shone—silent and beautiful!

Before them lay their path through the wide world—

The nightingales were singing as they pass'd;

And, looking back upon the glimm'ring tow'rs,

THEY, led by Ailric, and with thoughts on Heav'n,

Through the lone forest held their pensive way!

<hr>

CONCLUSION.

WILLIAM, on his imperial throne at York

Is seated, clad in steel, all but his face,

From casque to spur.   His brow yet wears a frown,

And his eyes show the unextinguish'd fire.

Of stedfast vengeance, as his inmost heart

Yet labour'd, like the ocean after storm.

His sword unsheath'd appears, which none beside

Can wield; his sable beard, full and diffus'd,

Below the casque is spread; the lion ramps

Upon his mailed breast, engrail'd with gold.

Behind him stand his barons, in dark file *

Rang'd, and each feature hid beneath the helms;

Spears, with escutcheon'd banners on their points,

Above their heads are rais'd.   Though all alike

Are cas'd in armour, know ye not that knight

Who next, behind the King, seems more intent

To listen, and a loftier stature bears?

'Tis bold Montgomerie; and he who kneels

Before the seat, his armour, all with gules,

Checker'd, and checker'd his small banneret,

Is Lord Fitz-alain. WILLIAM holds a scroll

In his right hand, and to Fitz-alain speaks:

" All these, the forfeited domains and land

" Of Edwin and of Morcar, traitor-lords,

* The picture is taken from an original, preserved in Drake, in which William and his barons are thus represented.   He is shown in the act of presenting his nephew Alain with the forfeited lands of Earl Edwin.

" From Ely to the banks of Trent, I give
" To thee and thine!"

       Fitz-alain lowly knelt,
And kiss'd his iron-hand, then slow arose,
Whilst all the Barons shouted, " LIVE THE KING!"

————————

This is thy song, WILLIAM THE CONQUEROR,
The tale of HAROLD's children, and THE GRAVE
OF THE LAST SAXON!   The huge fortress frowns
Still on the Thames, where WILLIAM's banner wav'd,
Though centuries, year after year, have pass'd,
As the stream flows for ever at its feet—
HAROLD, thy bones are scatter'd, and the tomb
That held them, where the Lea's lorn wave delay'd*,
Is seen no more; and the high fane, that heard
The ELEESON pealing for thy soul,
A fragment stands, and none will know the spot
Where those, whom thou didst love, in dust repose,
Thy CHILDREN!——But the tale may not be vain,

   * " Waltham" is, literally, the Ham in the Wold.

If haply it awake one duteous thought
Of filial tenderness.

That day of blood
Is pass'd, like a dark spectre! but it speaks
Ev'n to the kingdoms of the earth—

" Behold

" The hand of God ! from that dark day of blood,

" When Vengeance triumph'd, and the curfew knoll'd,

" England, thy proud majestic policy

" Slowly arose! through centuries of shade

" The pile august of British liberty

" Tower'd, till behold it stand in clearer light

" Illustrious.   At its base fell Tyranny

" Gnashes his teeth, and drops the broken sword ;

" Whilst Freedom, Justice, to the cloudless skies

" Uplift their radiant forms, and Fame aloft

" Sounds o'er the subject seas, from East to West,

" From North to South, her trumpet—' ENGLAND, LIVE !

" ' AND RULE, TILL WAVES AND WORLDS SHALL BE NO
    MORE !' "

NOTES.

Page 6, line 16.
Every trace has vanish'd.
Part of the abbey remains, but I believe there is no trace of the tomb; it was of gray marble. That part of the abbey where it lay is entirely destroyed.

Page 7, line 12.
Where Lea.
The river Lea, near which the abbey called Waltham Holy Cross was founded.

Page 8, line 16.
Marcus.
I have taken the liberty, for the sake of euphony, to alter the name of Harold's third son, from Magnus to Marcus.

There is a quaint epitaph in Speed, describing him as having been buried in a convent at Lewes. I have so far adhered to historical tradition, as to represent him under the character and in the habit of a religious order. The abbey, founded by his father, seemed more appropriate than a convent or cell at Lewes. The wife of Harold is not introduced at the funeral, as she had fled to a convent.

Page 9, line 12.
Leofrine.

Altered from the real name, for the same cause as I have given a variation to the name of Magnus.   I have taken the liberty also of representing the " religious" at Waltham Abbey as Monks; though, in fact, they were " Canons."

Page 10, line 11.
Spurn-head.

Spurn-head, at the entrance of the Humber.

Page 11, line 14.
Like the two brothers famed in ancient song.

Fratres Helenæ.

HORACE.

Page 12, line 9.
Ravenspur.

This town and castle are now vanished; but the name is well known in English history.   It is uncertain whether it was built since the Conquest, but there can be no doubt there was a castle at the entrance of the Humber; and as the name was familiar, and the antiquity of the place acknowledged, I consider myself at liberty to retain the name.

Page 27, line 3.
Red portentous comet.

A comet appeared at the time of Harold's coronation.

Page 27, line 10.
Fierce Norwegian.

Hardrada, of Norway, had invaded England just before

the arrival of William. Harold defeated him with immense slaughter in the north, and was called from thence to a more desperate and fatal struggle.

Page 30, line 17.
A hundred Norman knights.

William and the Normans were solicitous to pay every mark of respect to the remains of the late king.

Page 33, line 14.
Panope.

———— On the level brine,
Sleek PANOPE, with all her sisters play'd.

MILTON.

Page 34, line 3.
The very swallows.

I have placed, according to the best accounts, the taking of York at the fall of the year.

William prepared his army, and took the field in the spring; and the whole country, north of the Humber to the Tyne, was entirely laid waste and desolated by fire, famine, and the sword. See Turner's excellent History of England, and of the Anglo-Saxons.

Page 36, line 17.
But o'er her child, a frantic mother.

Only one family was saved in the massacre of the Normans at York. The name is Malet, or Mallet. I have made this historical circumstance illustrative of the milder, but no less brave, character of Edmund, and introduced the episode for the sake of " relief;" as many other descriptions, which I need not point out.

Page 42, line 6.
First, within the Tower.

Whether it is a matter of fact or not, that the Tower was finished in this year, I am justified in assuming it poetically, and it is at least historically credible.

Page 43, line 19.
London's sole Tow'r might laugh their strength to scorn.
" Our Castle's strength will laugh a siege to scorn."
Macbeth.

Page 44, line 7.
Yet calm his countenance.

William, with all his sternness, is described by contemporary historians as having a remarkable complacent smile, and seems to have been by nature bold, benevolent, and superstitious. I have endeavoured to sketch his portrait, as it appears from a comparison of the writers of the period.

ILLUSTRATIONS FROM SPEED.

" This victory thus obtained Duke William wholly ascribed vnto God, and by way of a solemne supplication or procession, gaue him the thankes; and pitching for that night his pauilion among the bodies of the dead, the next day returned to Hastings, there to consult vpon his great and most prosperously begun enterprise, giuing first commandement for the buriall of his slain souldiers.

' But Morcar and Edwin, the vnfortunate Queenes Brethren, by night escaping the battaile, came vnto London, where, with the rest of the Peeres, they beganne to lay the foundation of some fresh hopes; posting thence their messengers to raise a new supply, and to comfort the English (who, through all the Land, were stricken into a fearefull astonishment with this vnexpected newes) from a despairing feare, shewing the chance of Warre to be mutable, their number many and Captaines sufficient to try another field. Alfred, Archbishop of Yorke, there present, and President of the Assembly, stoutly and prudently gaue his counsell forthwith to consecrate and crowne young Edgar Atheling (the true heire) for their King, to whom consented likewise both the sea-Captaines and the Londoners. But the Earles of Yorkeshire and Cheshire, Edwin and Morcar (whom this fearefull state of their country could not disswade from disloyaltie and ambition), plotting secretly to get the crown themselues, hindred that wise and noble designe. In which, while the sorrowfull Queene, their sister, was conueyed to Westchester, where, without state or title of a Queene, she led a solitary and quiet life.

" The Mother of the slaine King did not so well moderate her womanly passions as to receiue either comfort or counsell of her friends: the dead body of her sonne shee greatly desired, and to that end sent to the Conquerour two sage brethren of his Abbey at Waltham, who had accompanied him in his vnfortunate expedition: Their names (as I finde them recorded in an olde manuscript) were Osegod and Ailric, whose message to the Conquerour, not without abundance of teares and feare, is there set downe in the tenour as followeth:

" ' Noble Duke ; and ere long to be a most great and mightie
King, we thy most humble seruants, destitute of all comfort
(as we would we were also of life) are come to thee as sent
from our brethren, whom this dead King hath placed in the
Monastery of Waltham, to attend the issue of this late dreadfull
battaile (wherein God fauouring thy quarrell, he is now taken
away and dead, which was our greatest comforter, and by
whose onely bountifull goodnesse we were relieued and main-
tained, whom hee had placed to serue God in that Church.)
Wherefore wee most humbly request the (now our dread
Lord) by that gracious fauour which the Lord of Lords hath
shewed vnto thee, and for the reliefe of their soules, who in
this quarrell haue ended their dayes, that it may be lawfull
for vs by thy good leaue safely to take and carry away with vs
the dead body of the King, the Founder and builder of our
Church and Monasterie ; as also the bodies of such others as
whom for the reuerence of him and for his sake desired also
to be buried with vs, that the state of our Church by their
helpe strengthened, may be the stronger, and indure the firmer.'
With whose so humble a request, and abundant teares, the
victorious and worthy Duke moued, answered :

" ' Your King (said he) vnmindfull of his faith, although
he haue for the present endured the worthy punishment of his
fault, yet hath he not therefore deserued to want the honour
of a Sepulchre or to lie vnburied : were it but that he dyed a
King, howsoeuer he came by the Kingdom, my purpose is, for
the reuerence of him and for the health of them who hauing
left their wiues and possessions haue here in my quarrel lost
their liues, to build here a Church and a monastery with an
hundred Monkes in it, to pray for them for euer, and in the
same Church to bury your King aboue the rest, with all ho-

hour vnto so great a Prince, and for his sake to endow the same with great reuenewes.'

" With which his courteous speech and promises, the two religious fathers, comforted and encouraged, again replied :

" ' Not so, noble Duke, but grant this thy servants most humble request, that we may, for God by the leaue, receiue the dead body of our Founder, and to bury it in the place which himself in his life time appointed, that wee, cheered with the presence of his body, may thereof take comfort, and that his Tombe may be vnto our successors a perpetual monument of his remembrance.'

" The Duke, as he was of disposition gracious, and inclined to mercy, forthwith granted their desires, whereupon they drew out stores of gold to present him in way of gratulation, which he not only vtterly refused, but also offered them plenty to supply whatsoeuer should be needfull for the pompe of his funerall, as also for their costs in trauaile to and fro, giuing strait commandments that none of his souldiers should persume to molest them in this businesse or in their returne. Then went they in haste to the quarry of the dead, but by no meanes could find the body of the King; for the countenances of all men greatly alter by death, but being maimed and imbrued with bloud, they are not known to be the men they were. As for his other regall ornaments which might haue shewed him for their King, his dead corps was despoyled of them, either through the greedy desire of prey (as the manner of the field is) or to be the first bringer of such happy news, in hope of a princely reward, vpon which purpose many times the body is both mangled and dismembred, and so was this King after his death by a base souldier gasht and hackt into the legge, whom Duke William rewarded for so vnsuldier like a deed, casheiring him for euer out of his wages and warres. So that Harold, lying stript, wounded, bemangled, and goared in his bloud, could not be founde nor knowne till they sent for a woman named Editha (for her passing beatie surnamed Swan shals, that is, Swans-necke), whom hee entertained in secret loue before he was King, who by some secret marks of his body, to her well knowne, found him out, and then put into a coffine, was by diuers of the Norman Nobilitie honourably brought vnto the place afterward called Battle Bridge, where it was met by the nobles of England, and, so conueyed to Waltham, was there solemnly and with great lamentation of his mother, royally interred, with this rude Epitaph *, well beseeming the time, though not the person.

" Goodwine, the eldest son of the King Harold, being growne to some ripenesse of years in yᵉ life of his Father, after his death and ouerthrow by the Conquerour, took his brother with him and flew ouer into Ireland, from whence he returned and landed in Somersetshire, slew Edmoth (a Baron sometimes of his Fathers) that encountered him, and taking great preyes in Deuonshire and Cornwell, and departed till the next yeare. When comeing again he fought with Beorn and Earle of Cornwall, and after retired into Ireland, and thence went into Denmarke to King Swayn, his Cosen German, where he spent the rest of his life.

" Edmund, the second sonne to King Harold, went with

* For this epitaph, see Speed.

his brother into Ireland, returned with him into England, and was at the slaughter and ouerthrow of Edmoth and his power in Sommesetshire, at the spoyles committed in Cornwall and Devonshire, at the conflict with the cornish Earle Beorn, passed, repassed with him in all his voyages, inuasions, and warres, by sea and by land, in England and Ireland; and at the last departed with him from Ireland to Denmarke, tooke part with him of all plasure and calamitie whatsoeuer, and attending and depending wholly upon him, liued and died with him in that country.

" Magnus, the third sonne of the King Harold, went with his brothers into Ireland, and returned with them the first time into England, and is neuer after that mentioned amongst them, nor elsewhere, vnlesse (as some coniecture) he be that Magnus, who, seeing the mutability of humane affaires, became an Anchoret, whose epitaph, pointing to his Danish originall, the learned Clarenciaux discouered in a little desolate Church at Lewes, in Sussex, where, in the gaping chinks of an arch in the wall, in a rude and ouer worne character, certain old imperfect verses were found."

A daughter, whose name is not known, left England with her brothers, and sought refuge with them in Denmark.

Speed quotes Saxo Grammaticus, who says, " She afterwards married Waldemar, King of Russia." To this daughter I have given the name and character in the poem.

THE END.

LONDON:

PRINTED BY THOMAS DAVISON, WHITEFRIARS.

ELLEN GRAY;

or,

THE DEAD MAIDEN'S CURSE.

J. MOYES, GREVILLE STREET, LONDON.

ELLEN GRAY;

OR,

THE DEAD MAIDEN'S CURSE.

A POEM,

BY THE LATE

DR. ARCHIBALD MACLEOD.

Omnibus umbra locis adero! — Virgil.

EDINBURGH:

PRINTED FOR ARCHIBALD CONSTABLE AND CO.;

AND HURST, ROBINSON, AND CO., 90, CHEAPSIDE,
AND 8, PALL MALL, LONDON.

1823.

TO

JOANNA BAILLIE,

𝔗𝔥𝔦𝔰 𝔖𝔪𝔞𝔩𝔩 𝔓𝔬𝔢𝔪,

FOUND AMONG THE PAPERS OF THE LATE

DR. ARCHIBALD MACLEOD,

IS RESPECTFULLY AND GRATEFULLY

𝔍𝔫𝔰𝔠𝔯𝔦𝔟𝔢𝔡,

BY THE EDITOR.

INTRODUCTION.

As some account of the origin of this Poem may be reasonably expected by the reader, the following brief memorial is prefixed, digested from a few unconnected hints and memoranda, contained in certain papers which Dr. Macleod had left behind him, at his lodgings, in the village of Mousehole, in Mount's Bay, Cornwall, where he had attached numerous friends, in his place of temporary sojournment, by his agreeable manners and interesting eccentricities.

The first glance at the notes of which we have just spoken, was sufficient to satisfy us that the Doctor had left Edinburgh, and travelled into the west of England, in search of the POETICAL: an idea which had probably been suggested to

his mind by the amusing details of another tra-
veller, the celebrated Doctor Syntax, some time
since given to the public, as the results of his
tour in search of the PICTURESQUE.

Be this, however, as it may, it is sufficiently
clear, from the papers above mentioned, that the
Doctor penetrated to the south-western extremity
of our island, with the intention of searching out,
and seizing upon, every floating tradition, local
superstition, and affecting incident, afforded by
the various counties through which he passed,
that appeared to be most adapted to his peculiar
pursuits.

Among the many local facts with which his
diligent investigation was rewarded, the ground-
work of the following Poem may be considered as
not one of the least interesting, — the plain narra-
tion of which is subjoined in the Appendix, taken
from the Rev. Mr. Polwhele's History of Corn-
wall.

Gratified as we ourselves have been with the

perusal of this production of Doctor Macleod's Muse, it is sufficiently known, that in these times attention is given, and praise awarded, *not* so much to *what is written*, as to *who it is that writes*.

Bare merit, in truth, without the fortunate adjunct of a *favourite name*, seems at present to have little chance of successful notoriety; led, or fettered, as the popular taste is, by the periodical publications of the day. A stranger has scarce a chance of *being heard*, among so many claimants, and where every bard (it might almost be said) has *his own critic*.

We tremble, indeed, for the fate of our author, so little known as Doctor Macleod is, when we perceive that the very *first line* of his poem may afford occasion for the exercise of that peculiar wit which often characterizes the tone of some of our periodical criticisms : *

" Oh, shut the book, dear Ellen! shut the book!"

---

* There are some manly and liberal exceptions.

May not the critic here facetiously exclaim,

" Oh, shut the book, dear *Reader!* shut the book!"

or inform the public, that the line is a mere plagiarism from **Pope**:

" Shut, shut the door, good John! fatigued, I said?"

It is not impossible, also, that some more important circumstances may call forth the critic's vituperation, — we mean, the *character* of the composition of the Poem, unaccommodated to the style and taste so much in fashion, and its total lack of all those glittering conceptions and dazzling expressions which are now the *sine quibus non* of popular poetry. Here are no " diamond tears " of sensibility; no " gems " of sparkling sentiment; no metaphorical gardens of Arcadia: and the Doctor has shown himself, in this effusion, either so lamentably ignorant of the choicest figures of rhetoric, or so conceitedly disdainful of such accessaries, as to neglect even that most important one, to which the modern sons of

Parnassus are so deeply indebted, the *catachresis*, by the aid of which, according to the scholastic definition of Martinus Scriblerus, " the grass is *shaved*, and the beard is *mown !*"

Of the leading motive of the Doctor's tour to the west, we have already spoken; it is necessary, however, to add, that, from particular poetical associations, he had an earnest desire to visit and contemplate that singular feature in the scenery of Cornwall, of high poetical interest,

" Michael's Mount and chair ;"

and, moreover, " debitâ spargere lacrymâ favillam" of Dolly Pentreath, with whom (according to the Hon. Daines Barrington) the faculty of speaking the ancient Cornish language expired. Of his visit to the former poetical spot, this Poem is the result.

In visiting the spot where this gifted female lies, among " th' unhonour'd dead " of her native village, the Doctor's curiosity, taste, and

feeling, were equally gratified, by discovering
and transcribing the curious inscription which
appears on the " frail memorial" that protects
her bones from insult, and which is couched
in the venerable language of the aboriginal
Britons. The lines are as follow, and will be
allowed to be in strict accordance with some
of the *simply pathetic* effusions of the present
day: —

> " Coth Doll Pentreath cans ha deau
> Morow ha bledyn ed Paul pleau,
> Na ed an egloz gan pobel bras,
> Bet ed egloz-hay coth Dolly es."

A quatrain of great beauty in the original (as the
multilinguists assert), and thus rendered, we have
no doubt with fidelity, by the historian of Dan-
monium: —

> " Old Doll Pentreath, one hundred aged and two,
> Deceas'd and buried in Paul's parish too;
> Not in the church, with people great and high,
> But in the churchyard does old Dolly lie."

The Doctor, unwilling probably that such a
tender composition should be confined to the
almost unintelligible original and its English
translation, made the following version of it into
Latin, for the general benefit of the learned; and
we really think, that he has not only admirably
hit off the style of the sepulchral inscriptions
preserved in Weaver, but also done ample justice
to the simplicity and pathos of Dolly's monu-
mental lines : —

" Nata annos plusquam centum annosissima Dolly
Hic jacet, heu! Pentreath, exteriore solo:
Non jacet illa, intra muros Pauli benedicti,
Cum summis, extra pauperibusque jacet."

To be serious, however, the version appears
to be merely a good-natured stroke of raillery on
some pathetic productions of a few poetical con-
temporaries, — and, indeed, the chief object of the
Doctor, in poetical style, appears to have been,
to show that taste lay between the Scylla and

Charybdis of *bombast* on the one hand, and affected *simplicity* and *puerility* on the other.

But, enough of our remarks : let the Doctor now speak for himself.

MARAZION, IN MOUNT'S BAY, CORNWALL,
March 5th, 1823.

THE " HOARY SWAIN " OF A WESTERN VILLAGE IS SUPPOSED TO
POINT TO A NAMELESS GRAVE, AND RELATE TO THE PASSENGER
THE TALE WHICH IS THE SUBJECT OF THIS POEM.

ELLEN GRAY;

OR,

THE MAIDEN'S CURSE!

" OH! SHUT THE BOOK, dear Ellen, shut the book!"
HUBERT exclaim'd, with wild and frantic look.—

She whom he lov'd was in her shroud,—nor pain
Nor grief shall visit her sad heart again.
There is no sculptur'd tomb-stone at her head;
No rude memorial marks her lowly bed:
The village children, every holiday,
Round the green turf, in summer sunshine play;
And none, but those now bending to the tomb,
Remember ELLEN, lovely in her bloom!

B

Yet oft the hoary swain, when autumn sighs
Thro' the long grass, sees a dim form arise,
(Its wan lips moving, in its hand a BOOK,)
And hie in glimmering moonlight to the brook.
So, like a bruised flower, when in the pride
Of youth and beauty, injur'd Ellen died.
Hubert some years surviv'd, but years no trace
Of his sick heart's deep anguish could erase.
Still the dread spectre seem'd to rise, and, worse,
Still in his ears rung the appalling CURSE,
(While loud he cries, despair upon his look,)
"OH! SHUT THE BOOK, DEAR ELLEN, SHUT THE BOOK!"

The sun is in the west; and the last ray
Yet lingers on our churchyard dial grey.
Come, sit on these stone steps, while I relate
Hubert's dread doom, and hapless Ellen's fate.

Yon tempest-shatter'd elm, that heavily
Sways to the wind, seems for the dead to sigh.

How many generations, since the day
Of its green pride, have pass'd, like leaves, away;
How many children of the hamlet play'd
Round its hoar trunk, who at its feet were laid,
Wither'd and grey old men! In life's first bloom,
How many has it seen borne to the tomb!
But never one so sunk in hopeless woe
As she, who in that nameless grave lies low.

HER, I remember, by her mother's chair,
Lisping, with folded hands, her first imperfect pray'r:
For Ellen grew, as beautiful in youth,
As lesson'd in the early lore of truth.
What diff'rent passions in her bosom strove,
When first she heard the tale of village love!
The youth whose voice then won her partial ear,
A yeoman's son, had pass'd his twentieth year;
She scarce eighteen: her mother, with the care
Of boding age, oft whisper'd, " Oh! beware!"
For HUBERT was a thoughtless youth, and wild,
And like a colt, unbroken from a child:

But he had vow'd, and plighted her his troth,
" Never to part;" and HEAVEN HAD HEARD THE OATH.

   Poor Ellen, while her father was alive,
Saw all things round the humble dwelling thrive:
Her widow'd mother now was growing old,
And, one by one, their worldly goods were sold:
Ellen remain'd, her mother's hope and pride ——
How oft, when she was sleeping by her side,
She wak'd at night, and kiss'd her brow, with tears,
And prayed for blessings on her future years,—
When she, her mother, ev'ry trial o'er,
Should rest on earth's cold lap, to weep no more.

   But Ellen to love's dream her heart resign'd,
And gave to fancy all her ardent mind.
Shall I describe her?— Did'st thou never mark
A soft blue light, beneath eye-lashes dark?
Hair auburn, part by riband-braid confin'd,
Part o'er her brow, blown lightly by the wind?

The village beauty, when on Sunday drest,

Her looks a sweet, but lowly grace express'd,

As modest as the violet at her breast.

She sat all day by her grey mother's side,

And now and then would turn a tear to hide.

Such Ellen was, in her youth's opening day,—

Now in the grave, and to the worm a prey.

Where winds the brook, by yonder bord'ring wood,

Her mother's solitary cottage stood.

A few pale poplars, and an aged pine,

Its rugged bark festoon'd with eglantine,

Grew near the whiten'd front, that, o'er the down,

Look'd to the grey smoke of a neighb'ring town.

Beneath an ivied bank, abrupt and high,

A small clear well reflected bank and sky,

In whose translucent mirror, smooth and still,

From time to time, a small bird dipp'd its bill.

Before the window, with late April show'rs
Refresh'd, a border bloom'd of Ellen's flow'rs.
There the first snow-drop; and, of livelier hue,
The polyanthus and narcissus grew.
'Twas Ellen's care a jessamine to train,
With small white blossoms round the window-pane:
A rustic wicket open'd to the meads,
Where a scant path-way to the hamlet leads:
A mill-wheel in the glen toil'd round and round,
Dashing the o'er-shot stream, with deep continuous
   sound.
Beyond, when the brief show'r had sail'd away,
The tap'ring spire shone out in sun-light grey;
And climb o'er yonder northern point, to sight
Stretching far on, the main-sea rolled in light.

 Enter the dwelling, it is small but neat,—
ONE BOOK lies open on the window-seat,—
The spectacles are on a leaf of JOB:
Here mark, a map of the terrestrial globe;

And opposite, with its prolific stem,

The Christian's tree*, and new Jerusalem;

Below, a printed paper to record

A veritable " LETTER FROM OUR LORD † :"

Some books are on the window-ledge beneath, —

The Book of Prayer, and Drelincourt on Death.

With sounds of birds and bees the garden rung,

And Ellen's linnet at the casement sung.

It is not long — not long to Whitsuntide,

And haply Ellen then shall be a bride.

On Sunday morn, when a slant light was flung

On the pale tow'r, where bells awak'ning rung,

Hubert and Ellen I have seen repair,

Arm link'd in arm, to the same house of pray'r.

" These bells will sound more merrily" (he cried,

And gently press'd her hand) " at Whitsuntide."

* Large, coloured prints, in most cottages.

† The letter said to be written by our Saviour, to king Agbarus.
This also is seen in many cottages.

She check'd th' intruding thought, and hung her head;
Ellen, alas! ere Whitsuntide — was dead!

'Twas said, but we could scarce the tale believe,
That Ellen's form was seen upon that eve *,
When, in the churchyard trooping, all appear,
All who should die within the coming year;
Piteous and strangely pallid was her look,   .
Her right hand held the shadow of a book,
On which her long hair dripp'd, — the cold moon cast
A glimmering light, as in her shroud she pass'd!
One thing is certain, that she went alone
To learn her fate, at Madern's mystic stone †;

* In Cornwall, and in other counties remote from the metropolis, it is a popular belief, that they who are to die in the course of the year, appear, on the eve of Midsummer, before the church porch. See an exquisite dramatic sketch on this subject, called " the Eve of St. Mark."

† Madern-stone, a Druidical monument in the village of Madern, to which the country people often resort, to learn their future destinies.

What there she heard ne'er came to human ears;
But, from that hour she oft was seen in tears.

'Twas spring tide now: the butterfly more bright,
Wheel'd o'er the cowslips, in the rainbow light;
The lamb, the colt, the blackbird in the brake,
Seem'd all a vernal feeling to partake;
The " swallow twitter'd" in the earliest ray,
That show'd the flow'r on Gwinnear's turret grey;
More grateful comes the fragrance after rain,
To him who steals along the sweet-briar lane,
And all things seem, to the full heart, to bring
The blissful breathings of the world's first spring.

More cheerful came the sunshine of MAY-MORN,
The bee from earliest light had wound his horn,
Busiest from flower to flower, as he would say,
" Up! Ellen! for it is the morn of May!"
The lads and lasses of the hamlet bore
Branches of blossom'd thorn or sycamore *;

* This is invariably the custom in Cornwall. See POLWHELE.

And at her mother's porch a garland hung,

While thus their rustic roundelay they sung : —

MAY SONG.

1.

" And we were up as soon as day*,

  " To fetch the summer home,

" The summer and the May,

  " For summer now is come."

2.

In Madern vale the bell-flow'rs bloom†,

  And wave to Zephyr's stirring breath:

The cuckoo sings in Morval coombe,

  O'er Penron spreads the purple heath‡.

* These are the first four lines of the real song of the season, which is called " the Furry-song of Helstone."

† Campanula cymbalaria, foliis hederaciis.

‡ Erica multiflora, common in this part of Cornwall.

3.

Come, dance around Glen-Alston tree,
    We 'll weave a crown of flowrets gay,
And ELLEN of the BROOK shall be
    Our LADY OF THE MAY.

ELLEN expected HUBERT; the first flow'r
She gather'd, now was fading; hour by hour
She watch'd the sunshine on the thatch; again
Her mother turn'd the hour-glass; now, the pane
The west'ring sun has left.   The long May-day,
So Ellen wore in hopes and fears away.
Slow twilight steals — by the small garden-gate
She stands, — " Oh! Hubert never came so late!"
Her mother's voice is heard; " Good child, come in;
" Dream not of bliss on earth — it is a sin :
" Come, take the BIBLE down, my child, and read;
" In disappointed hopes, in grief, in need, —
" By friends forsaken, and by fears oppress'd,
" *There*, only, can the weary heart find rest!"

Her thin hands mark'd by many a wand'ring vein,
The mother turn'd her ebbing glass again;
The rush-light now is lit—the Bible read,—
But, ere poor ELLEN can retire to bed,
She listens,—Hark! no voice, no step she hears,—
Oh! seek thy bed to hide those bursting tears!

When the slow morning came, the tale was told,
(Need it have been?) that Hubert's love was cold.

But hope yet whispers, " Dry the accusing tear,—
When SUNDAY comes, again he will be here!"
And Sunday came, and struggling from a cloud,
The sun shone bright, — the bells were chiming loud,—
And lads and lasses in their best attire,
Were tripping past, and light was on the spire;—
But HUBERT came not; — with an aching heart
Poor ELLEN saw the Sunday train depart:
Her mother follow'd, with starch'd pinners clean,
And pray'r-book, tottering o'er the dewy green;

Ellen, to hear no more of peace on earth,
Retir'd in silence to the lonely hearth.

Next day the tidings to the cottage came,
That Hubert's heart confess'd another flame:
That, cold and wayward falsehood made him prove
At once a TRAITOR to his FAITH and LOVE;
That, with our Bailiff's daughter he was seen,
At the new Tabernacle on the green;
Had join'd the Calvinistic flock, and there
Renounc'd his PRAY'R-BOOK, yea, our SAVIOUR's PRAY'R*;

* The poet is unhappily borne out in this incident, by the *actual fact* of the rejection of the LORD's PRAYER and TEN COMMANDMENTS, in the service of certain places of dissenting worship. It is in the recollection of our readers, that during the course of last year, a witness appeared to give evidence in one of our courts of justice, who had *constantly attended* a *place* of *worship* with her mother, but *never heard* of the *Lord's Prayer*, or the *Ten Commandments*: the judge, very properly, refused to admit her evidence, until she had been six months under the instruction of a clergyman of the Church of England. Such a fact speaks volumes, and may be considered as a practical comment upon an expression of Bunyan, in his " Pilgrim's Progress," who calls going to church, *going to the town of morality.*

The Doctor, in the lines to which this note refers, cannot be sup-

And, if he left young Ellen's heart to bleed,
Poor Ellen's heart to break — IT WAS DECREED!

Alas! her heart was left indeed to break;
Wan sorrow prey'd upon her vermeil cheek. —
Now, with a ghastly moodiness she smil'd,
Now, still and placid look'd as when a child,
Or rais'd her eyes disconsolate and wild.

Then, as she stray'd the brook's green marge along,
She oft would sing this sad and broken song: —

1.

Lay me where the willows wave,
    In the cold moon-light;
Shine upon my quiet grave,
    Softly, queen of night!

posed to allude to the philosophical, or at least sober, Calvinism of
the Scotch and Genevan churches; but to the *vulgar* and *terrible*
Calvinism mouthed out by the ignoramuses, enthusiasts, or something
worse, of some of our own conventicles.

2.

I to thee would fly for rest,
But a stone — a stone —
Lies like lead upon my breast,
All hope on earth is flown.

3.

Lay me where the willows wave,
In the cold moon-light;
Shine upon my quiet grave,
Softly, queen of night * !

Her mother said, " My child, go unconfin'd,
" For thou art meek and harmless, and thy mind
" The water's sound may soothe; or, as it blows,
" The very tempest bring thy mind repose."

* The cadence of this song is taken from a ballad " most musical, most melancholy," in the British tragedy, " Lay a garland on my grave."

Ellen oft wander'd to the northern shore *,

And heard, with boding voice, the gaunt TREGAGEL† roar,

Among the rocks, and when the tempest blew,

And like the shivered foam her long hair flew,

And all the billowy space was tossing wide,

" Rock! rock! thou melancholy main," she cried,

" I love thy noise, oh, ever sounding sea,

" And learn stern patience, while I look on thee!"

    Then on the clouds she gazed with vacant stare,

Or dancing with wild fennel in her hair‡,

Sang merrily : " Oh! we must dry the tear,

" For Mab, the queen of fairies, will be here,—

* The bay of St. Ives.

† Tregagel is a giant, whose voice (according to the superstition of the country) is heard among the rocks constantly preceding and during a storm.

‡ Feniculum vulgare, or wild fennel, common on the northern coast of Cornwall.

She shall know all — know all,"—and then again
Her ditty died into its opening strain : —

> " Lay me where the willows wave,
>   In the cold moon-light;
> Shine upon my quiet grave,
>   Softly, queen of night!"

The children in their sports would pause and say *,
With pitying look, " There goes poor Ellen Gray."

Now, loitering home, while tears ran down apace,
She look'd in silence in her mother's face;
Then, starting up, with wild emotion cried,
" To-morrow! oh, to-morrow's Whitsuntide,
" And all shall dance when Ellen is a bride!"

* Who does not remember Crabbe's exquisite lines in his Village,
and the affecting image of the children standing over the old man's
grave?—
    " Silent and sad, and gazing hand in hand!"

C

Now, some dire thought seem'd in her heart to rise,
Stern with terrific joy she roll'd her eyes:
Her mother heeded not, — nor when she took
(With more impatient haste) her Sunday book, —
She heeded not — for age had dimmed her sight.

Now twilight slowly steals — 'tis eve — 'tis night, —
" ELLEN ! my ELLEN !" her lone mother cried,
" ELLEN ! my ELLEN !" — but NO VOICE REPLIED.

CANTO II.

———

At early dawn, gay HUBERT pass'd along, —
The birds were singing loud their hedge-row song ; —
The meadow's pathway, on' which fairies threw
Their lightest net-work of the film and dew,
Careless he brush'd : the sun rose as he pass'd,
A line of glory on the scene was cast, —
Where the brook, trembling in the orient light,
Stole by ; and now, the small spire rose in sight,
As the mist creeping from the nether plain
Flew off, departing to the northern main.
Now, peeping from the river's farther side,
Ellen's maternal cottage he descried,
And saw a faded garland at the door,
And with'ring branches of the sycamore :

But heard no humming wheel, and saw no smoke
Slow rising o'er the shades of pine and oak.
Ah! was it fancy? as he pass'd along,
He thought he heard a spirit's feeble song*!
Struck by the thrilling sound, he turned his look,—
Upon the ground there lay an open BOOK,—
The page was folded down:—Spirit of grace!
Ah! there are soils, like tear-blots, on the place:
It was a PRAY'R-BOOK!—and these words he read:
" Let him be desolate, and beg his bread†!

* It is a common idea in Cornwall, that when any person is
drowned, the voice of his spirit may be heard by those who first
pass by.
† The passage folded down was the 109th Psalm, commonly called
" the imprecating Psalm." It is now generally understood, that the
imprecations were denounced by David's enemies against himself. I
extract the most affecting passages:—
" May his days be few."
" Let his children be fatherless, and his wife a widow."
" Let there be none to extend mercy."
" Let their name be blotted out, because he slayed even the broken
in heart."

" Let there be none—not one on earth to bless,—

" Be his days few,—his children fatherless,—

" His wife a widow!—let there be no friend

" In his last moments mercy to extend!"

It was a PRAY'R-BOOK he before had seen:

Where? when? Once more, wild terror on his mien,

He read the page:—" An outcast let him lie,

" And unlamented and deserted die!

" When he has children, may they pine away

" Before his sight,—to hopeless grief a prey!

" His wife――――"

He trembled—who could read unmov'd?

Ah! 'tis the written name of her he lov'd:—

" The BOOK OF ELLEN GRAY;—WHEN THIS YOU SEE,

" AND I AM DEAD AND GONE—REMEMBER ME!"

His limbs—they shake—the dew is on his brow:—

" THE CURSE IS HERS!—oh God! I FEEL IT NOW!

" I see already—ev'n at my right hand—

" POOR ELLEN, thy ACCUSING SPIRIT stand!

" I feel thy deep, last curse!" Then with a cry,
He sunk upon the earth in agony.

    Feebly he rose,—when, on the matted hair
Of a drown'd maid, and on her bosom bare,
The sun shone out; and, 'mid the sedges green,
Poor Ellen's cold and floating corse was seen.
" Merciful God !" with faltering voice he cries,
" Hide me ! oh, hide me from the sight! Those eyes—
" They glare on me! ob, hide me with the dead !
" THE CURSE — THE DEEP CURSE rests upon my head !"

    ELLEN, FAREWELL ! 'twas frenzy fir'd thy breast,—
That prompted horrors not to be express'd :
Whilst ever at thy side the foul fiend stood,
And, laughing, pointed to the oblivious flood.

    HUBERT, heart-stricken—to despair a prey,
Soon left the village, journeying far away;

But first, if signs his future fate might tell,

He sought the spirit of St. Cuthbert's well*:

He dropp'd a pebble — mark! no bubble bright

Follow'd; and slow he turn'd away his sight.

He look'd again: " Oh, God! those eye-balls glare,

" How terribly! ah, smooth that matted hair, —

" Ellen! dead Ellen! thy cold corse I see

" Rise from the fountain! look not thus at me!

" I cannot bear the sight — that form — that look!

" OH! SHUT THE BOOK, DEAR ELLEN, SHUT THE BOOK!"

Meantime, poor Ellen in the grave was laid; —

Her lone and grey-hair'd mother wept and pray'd:

Soon to the dust she follow'd; and unknown,

There, they both rest without a name or stone.

* The people of the country consult the spirit of the well for their future destiny, by dropping a pebble into it, striking the ground, and other methods of divination, derived, no doubt, from Pagan antiquity.— POLWHELE.

Pity them, pensive stranger, nòr pass by,
Till thou hast said one pray'r, for charity!

But what of Hubert? " Hide me in the mine !"
He cried, " the beams of day insulting shine !
" Earth's very shadows are too gay, too bright, —
" Hide me, for ever, in forgetful night!"
In vain; — that shade, the cause of all his woes,
More sternly terrible in darkness rose!
Nearer he saw, with its white waving hand,
That phantom in appalling stillness stand;
The letters in the book shone through the night,
More blasting! " Hide, oh hide me from the sight !
" Vast ocean, to thy solitudes I bring
" A heart, that not the fragrance of the spring, —
" The green-leaves' music, — or the wood-lark's strain, —
" Shall ever wake to hope or joy again!
" Ocean, be mine, — wild as thy wastes, to roam
" From clime to clime! — OCEAN, BE THOU MY HOME!"

Some said he died, — but he was seen no more ; —
He went to sea; yet there, amid the roar
Of the wild waters, starting from his sleep,
He gaz'd upon the lone tempestuous deep ;
When, slowly rising from the vessel's lee,
A shape appeared, which none besides could see;
And then he shriek'd, like one whom Heav'n forsook, —
"OH! SHUT THE BOOK, DEAR ELLEN, SHUT THE BOOK!"

In foreign lands, in darkness and in light,
The same dread spectre stood before his sight;
If slumber came, his aching lids to close,
Funereal forms in sad procession rose.
Sometimes he dreamed that ev'ry grief was pass'd, — .
Ellen had long been lost — was found at last, —
And now she smil'd as when in early life, —
The morn was come when she should be his wife;
The maids were dress'd in white, and all were gay,
And the bells rang for Ellen's wedding-day !

Then, wherefore sad? a chill comes o'er his soul,—
Hark! the glad bells have sunk into a toll,—
A slow, deep toll; and lo! a sable train
Of mourners, moving to the village fane.
A coffin now is laid in holy ground,
That, heavily, returns its hollow sound,
When the first earth upon its lid is thrown:
The hollow sound is chang'd into a groan:
And, rising with wan cheek, and dripping hair,
And moving lips, and eyes of ghastly stare,
A figure issues! Ah! it comes more near!
'Tis Ellen! and that BOOK with many a tear
Is wet, which, with her fingers long and cold,
He sees her to the glimmering moon unfold.
Her icy hand is laid upon his heart;
Gasping, he wakes,—and, with a convulsive start,
He gazes round.   Moonlight is on the tide—
The passing keel is scarcely heard to glide,—
Ah! there the spectre goes: with frenzied look
He shrieks, "OH! SHUT, DEAR ELLEN, SHUT THE BOOK!"

Now to the ocean's verge the phantom flies, —
And hark! far off, the lessening laughter dies.

Years roll'd away, — till now, at evening's close,
Faint, and more faint, th' ACCUSING SPIRIT rose.

Restor'd from toil, and perils of the main,
Now HUBERT treads his native land again.

Near the " hoar " mount, by Marazion's shore,
Where, from the west, Atlantic surges roar,
Where once, above the solitary main,
The MIGHTY VISION sat, and look'd to Spain*,
He liv'd, a lonely stranger, sad, but mild;
All mark'd the sadness, chiefly when he smil'd;

* The apparition of St. Michael, who, from the top of the mount so
called, as Milton says, in his Lycidas,

> " Looks to Namanco's and Bayonna's hold."

See a masterly note of T. Warton's on the passage, in illustration of its
imagery.

Some competence he gain'd, by years of toil:

So, in a cottage, on his native soil,

He dwelt, remote from crowds, nor told his tale

To human ear: he saw the white clouds sail

O'er the bright bay, when suns of summer shone,

And oft he wander'd, mutt'ring and alone.

He never went to church, where he might hear

The judgment-psalm, so harrowing to his ear:

The Bible on the window-seat was laid,

He wept upon it, and in secret pray'd;

But never join'd the social sabbath bands,

That to St. Paul's* pass'd o'er the whit'ning sands.

No other friend had he, save one blue jay†,

Which, from the Mississippi, far away,

O'er the Atlantic, to his native land

He brought;—it fed from its protector's hand,

---

* The village of St. Paul.

† The blue jay of the Mississippi. See Chateaubriand's Indian song, in Atala.

And sometimes sang at morn, so loud and clear,
That ev'ry passenger would pause to hear.
In the great world there was not one beside
For whom he car'd, since his grey father died.

Still manly strength was his, for thirteen years
Weigh'd light upon his frame, though pass'd in tears;
Not thirty-five his age, and in his face
There was of care, more than of time, the trace.

Ellen was half-forgotten; by degrees,
The sights and sounds of life began to please.

The widow'd Ruth in early life had known
Domestic griefs and losses of her own.
She — patient, mild, compassionate, and kind —
Waken'd to human sympathies his mind.
The first that won his notice, was her child,
Who fed his bird, and took his hand, and smil'd.
Ruth and her little boy, to most unknown,
Liv'd in a cottage that adjoin'd his own;

Oft, when the winds arose, by one small light

They read the Bible, on a Sabbath night.

The cottage look'd upon the circling bay;

Penzance, a streak of light, to southward lay;

Eastward the Lizard's hazy point was seen,

Now vanish'd in " a momentary spleen*;"

Nearer, the lone, romantic rock† uprears

Its tower'd brow, which like a crown appears,

And seems the shadow of its state to throw

Along the restless waves that break below.

Who has not sigh'd for the lone fisher's life,

So fraught with terror to an anxious wife?

Night after night, expos'd upon the main;

Returning tir'd with toil, or drench'd in rain;

His gains uncertain as his life, — he knows

No stated hours of labour and repose.

On land, when busy scenes of life retire,

And his wife looks upon the evening fire,

* " How is it vanish'd in a hasty spleen !"
      CROWE's Lewesden Hill, one of the finest poems of the age.
† St. Michael's Mount, with the Castle, &c.

He, afar off, 'mid the tempestuous night,
Haply, is thinking of that social light.

Ruth's husband left the bay, — the wind and rain
Came down, — the tempest swept the southern main ; —
Whether his skiff on some black shore was cast,
Or, whelm'd, he slept beneath the ocean vast,
Was never known ; — but, from his native shore,
Thy husband, Ruth, sail'd, — and return'd no more.
Seven years had pass'd, — and after evening pray'r,
To Hubert's cottage Ruth would oft repair,
And with her little son full late would stay,
Listening to tales of regions far away.
The wond'ring boy lov'd of wild scenes to hear ;
Of battles of the roving buccaneer ;
Of wild-fires lighted in the forest glen,
And songs and dances of the savage men ;
Then the pale mother would sit by and weep,
While Hubert told the dangers of the deep.
He spoke of many a peril he had pass'd, —
Of howling night-fiends riding on the blast, —

Of those, who, lonely and of hope bereft,

Upon some melancholy rock are left,

Who mark, despairing, at the close of day,

Perhaps, some far-off vessel sail away.

He spoke with pity of the land of slaves —

Then, of the phantom-ship that rides the roaring waves *.

It comes! it comes! A melancholy light

Gleams from the prow upon the storm of night.

'Tis here! 'tis there! In vain the billows roll;

It steers right on, — but not a living soul

Is there, to guide its voyage thro' the dark,

Or spread the sails of that terrific bark.

He spoke of vast sea-serpents, how they float

For many a rood, or near some hurrying boat

Lift up their tall neck, with a hissing sound †,

And turn their blood-shot eye-balls questing round.

* Called the flying Dutchman; the phantom ship of the Cape.

† The Doctor evidently seems here to have endeavoured to make the sound an echo to the sense.

" So Ajax strives," &c. — ESSAY ON CRITICISM.

He spoke of sea-maids, on the desert rocks,
Who in the sun comb their green, dripping locks,
While, heard at distance, in the parting ray,
Beyond the farthest promontory grey,
Aërial music swells and dies away!

　One night, they longer stay'd the tale to hear,
And Ruth that night " beguil'd him of a tear,
" When he did speak of the distressful stroke
" Which his youth suffer'd."　Then, she pitying spoke,
Yet placed RELIGIOUS HOPE within his view!
And from that night a tenderer feeling grew.
And why not, ere the long night of the dead,
Life's slow descending steep together tread?
Partake its transient light, or gathering gloom,
And journey gently onward to the tomb?

　The day was fix'd; no longer he shall roam,
But BOTH shall have ONE HEART, one house, ONE HOME:

D

The world shut out, BOTH shall together pray,
BOTH wait the evening of life's changeful day:
SHE shall his anguish soothe, when he grows wild, —
And HE shall be a FATHER TO HER CHILD.

Fair rose the dawn — the summer air how bland!
The blue wave scarcely seem'd to touch the land, —
So soft it lay, far off, in morning light,
Whilst here and there a scatter'd sail shone white.

Come, hasten — yonder is the church; away
All cares, for who can mournful be to-day?
The bells are ringing, and the rites are o'er, —
The nuptial train return along the shore,
Cheer'd by new hopes of life: as thus they pass'd,
In sudden blackness rush'd the impetuous blast *;
Deep thunder roll'd, with long portentous sound,
At distance: nearer now, it shakes the ground,

* Sudden storms are very common in this bay.

Whilst Hubert sinks with speechless dread oppress'd,
As the fork'd flash seems darted at his breast.
His beating heart was heard,—bleach'd was his cheek,—
A WELL-KNOWN VOICE seem'd in the storm to speak;
Aghast he cried, wild phrenzy in his look,
"OH! SHUT THE BOOK, DEAR ELLEN, SHUT THE BOOK!"

My tale is well-nigh o'e.; for, from that day,
(The arrow in his soul,) he pin'd away,
And silent sunk beneath the ceaseless smart
Of a PIERCED CONSCIENCE, and a BROKEN HEART.

Go, STRANGER, and instruct the YOUNG and FAIR;
Bid them of rash and hasty trust beware,
Lest they should find the dream for ever fly —
The dream of hope — and broken-hearted die!

And THOU, if ever thou hast prov'd unkind,
Or caus'd one sorrow to a virtuous mind;

If thou hast lov'd " some gentle maid and true,"

Whose first affections never swerv'd from you;

If thou hast seen with tears her eyelid swell,

When thou hast said — but for a time — FAREWELL!

LEAVE HER NOT — (oh! for pity and for ruth) —

LEAVE HER NOT " tearful in her days of youth *;"

For life may long, and not unhappy prove,

But ITS BEST BLESSING is — THE HEART'S FIRST LOVE!†

---

* " Tearful in the days of her youth." OSSIAN.

† The Doctor seems to have been so perverse in taste, as to think
that the humblest poem ought to have something of a *moral lesson.*

APPENDIX.

A LOOSE paper contained the following extract from Polwhele's History of Cornwall. The judicious reader will immediately acknowledge the good sense of the Doctor, in departing so far from the real fact, as to avoid describing Ellen dying under the influence of the dire and deliberate vindictiveness, which the unfortunate young woman in the story actually did. Instead of such a revolting representation, he wisely describes Ellen's selection of the imprecating psalm, and her act of suicide, as the effects of mental derangement, and the phrenzy of the MOMENT, when the sight of the PRAYER-BOOK awakened the most painful recollections, and excited the desperate, but *instant* idea.

A comparison, also, of the plain narrative with the poetical story, will enable the reader to perceive the variations, incidents, and ornaments, adopted by the Doctor, for the sake of poetical beauty and pathetic effect.

" October, 1780. Thomas Thomas, aged 37. This man died of mental anguish, or what is called a broken heart. He lived in the village of Drannock, in the parish of Gwinnear, till an unhappy event occurred, which proved fatal to his peace of mind, for more than eight years, and finally occasioned his death. He courted Elizabeth Thomas, of the same village, who was his first-cousin; and it was understood that they were under a matrimonial engagement. But in May, 1772, some little disagreement having happened between them, he, out of resentment, or from some other motive, paid great attention to another girl; and on Sunday, the 31st of that month, in the afternoon, accompanied her to the Methodist meeting at Wall. During their absence, the discarded female, who was very beautiful in her person, but of an extremely irritable temper, took a rope and a common prayer-book, in which she had folded down the 109th Psalm, and, going into an adjacent field, hanged herself. Thomas, on his return from the preaching, inquired for Betsy; and being told she had not been seen for two or three hours, he exclaimed, " Good God! she has destroyed herself!" which apprehension seems to show, either that she had threatened to commit suicide in consequence of his desertion, or that he dreaded it from a knowledge of the violence of her disposition. But when he saw that his fears were realized, and had read the psalm, so full of execrations, which she had pointed out to him, he cried out, " I am ruined for ever and ever!" The very sight of this village and neighbourhood was now become insupportable, and he went to live at Marazion, hoping that a change of scene and social inter-course might expel those excruciating reflections which harrowed up his very soul, or at least render them less acute; but in this he appeared to be mistaken, for he found himself closely pursued by the evil demon—

' Despair, whose torments no man, sure,
But lovers and the damn'd endure.'

" To hear the 109th Psalm would petrify him with horror, and therefore he would not attend divine service on the 22d day of the month; he dreaded to go near a reading school, lest he should hear the ill-fated lesson. Whatever misfortunes befel him (and these were not a few, for he was several times hurt, and even maimed in the mines where he laboured), he still attributed them all to the malevolent agency of the deceased, and thought he could find allusions to the whole in the calamitous legacy which she had bequeathed him. When he slumbered, for he knew nothing of sound sleep, the injured girl appeared to his imagination, with such a countenance as she had after the rash action, and the prayer-book in her hand, open at the hateful psalm; and he was frequently heard to cry out, " Oh, my dear Betsy, shut the book, shut the book!" &c. With a mind so disturbed and deranged, though he could not reasonably expect much consolation from matrimony, yet imagining that the cares of a family might draw off his thoughts from the miserable subject by which he was harassed both by day and night, he successively paid his addresses to many girls of Marazion; but they indignantly flew from him, and with a sneer asked him, whether he was desirous of bringing all the curses in the 109th Psalm on their heads? At length, however, he succeeded with one

who had less superstition and more fortitude than the
rest, and he led her to St. Hilary church, to be married,
January 21st, 1778; but on the road thither they were
overtaken by a sudden and violent hurricane, such as
those which not unfrequently happen in the vicinity of
Mount's Bay; and he, suspecting that poor Betsy rode
in the whirlwind and directed the storm, was convulsed
with terror, and was literally ' coupled with fear.'   Such
is the power of conscious guilt to impute accidental
occurrences to the hand of vindictive justice, — and so
true is the observation of the poet,

' Judicium metuit sibi mens mali conscia justum.'

" He lived long enough to have a son and a daughter;
but the corrosive worm within his breast preyed upon his
vitals, and at length consumed all the powers of his body,
as it had long before destroyed the tranquillity of his
mind, and was released from all his pangs, both mental
and corporeal, on Friday, October 20th, 1780, and buried
at St. Hilary, the Sunday following, during evening
service." — POLWHELE.

LONDON : — PRINTED BY J. MOYES, GREVILLE STREET.

RARY OF DAVI... ...OLL...